MW00875743

The Feminine Empowerment Plan

Five Steps to Achieve Personal Growth for Women in Their 20s

Kay Bagel

Kay Bagel Publishing

contained within this document, including, but not limited to, errors, omissions, or inaccuracies.

Introduction

There was a time when I used to sit in my room and go through my Instagram feed all day. I couldn't help but feel uneasy as I looked at post after post of my friends and acquaintances who seemed to be leading the lives of their dreams while I was still trying to figure out what I wanted from life. They were traveling the world, obtaining their ideal careers, and just seemed like they had everything planned out.

I felt like I had so much to accomplish, but I just didn't know how. I had high aspirations for myself but no strategy for achieving them. I also had a deep inkling that I wasn't alone in feeling this way. After all, studies reveal that many women in their 20s share this sense of apathy and uncertainty about the future.

This feeling I had in my early 20s is what slowly

sparked my interest in personal development. It led me to the breakthroughs I had in my mentality and in my personal life and career.

For women in their 20s, personal development is the process of self-improvement, self-discovery, and self-awareness that results in a sense of fulfillment and empowerment. As we journey from adolescence to adulthood, young women explore their identities, values, and purposes. The foundation for women's future success, well-being, and happiness is laid during this stage, so it is crucial for us to achieve personal growth.

Feminine empowerment plays a vital role in enabling young women to achieve personal growth. It involves creating an environment that fosters women's growth and development, allowing us to challenge gender stereotypes and overcome barriers that limit our potential. Feminine empowerment provides young women with the necessary tools, resources, and support to develop their skills, talents, and abilities. This enables them to become self-reliant and confident individuals.

Personal growth and feminine empowerment work hand in hand, as you cannot achieve the former without the latter. We need to feel empowered to take charge of our lives, pursue our passions, and make our own decisions. Feminine empowerment helps women break free from societal norms and expectations that restrict our potential, enabling us to embrace our uniqueness and individuality.

Many of us women in our 20s feel like we're not living up to our full potential. We feel held back by societal expectations, self-doubt, or lack of direction. Women like us struggle to find our footing in the world and navigate the challenges that come with this transformative decade.

We may face specific challenges related to our age and life stage, such as navigating early career challenges, managing relationships, or defining our identity. Feminine empowerment can provide support and guidance in these areas, helping us women to build our confidence and develop the skills and knowledge needed to succeed.

Achieving personal growth and feminine empowerment is not just about individual success, but also about creating a more equitable and just society. By empowering women to reach their full potential, we can create a world where everyone has the opportunity to prosper.

My name is Kay Bagel, and for the last five years, I've dedicated myself to researching self-help, personal growth, and women's empowerment. Equipped with this knowledge, I hope that my expertise and enthusiasm will make me the ideal mentor for your own journey of personal development and transformation.

As a woman in her mid-20s, I understand the unique challenges that women in their 20s face. I have been through many of the struggles you are going through right now, and have come out wiser, stronger, and more empowered than ever before.

Through my own experiences and the insights I have gained along the way, I have developed a powerful set of tools and strategies for personal growth that I'm eager to share with other young women to help them reach their full potential.

The Feminine Empowerment Plan is my way of guiding women in their 20s into a more fulfilling life by tapping into their feminine power and achieving personal growth. This guide is not just about a theoretical concept but a practical one that offers actionable steps to take in your life. My plan is not just about attaining external success but about finding inner peace and self-love.

My focus is on our imperative need to break free from a cycle of confusion and self-doubt. It's a roadmap specifically tailored to women in their 20s, providing a way to tap into our full potential and create the life we truly desire through personal growth and empowerment.

We'll begin by exploring the concept of femininity

and how it has been historically defined. I've learned that it's important to challenge traditional notions of femininity and embrace the unique strengths that come with feminine energy. It's also imperative to value self-love and self-care, which can help you create a life that aligns with your values and passions. In this book, you'll be challenged to take charge of your life and embrace your unique talents and abilities.

The Feminine Empowerment Plan is a holistic approach to personal growth that considers the unique challenges and opportunities that come with being a young woman. In this journey, you will discover the power of self-care and self-love, and how to cultivate these qualities in your own lives. I hope to teach you how to tap into your own strength, resilience, and intuition to overcome obstacles and achieve your goals. You will also learn how to set boundaries, communicate effectively, and build healthy relationships.

I hope that with my inspiration and ideas, you will discover parts of you that will transform you into the best version of yourself. So if you're tired of feeling stagnant and unfulfilled, join me on this journey to self-transformation, empowerment, and happiness.

Part One
The Perfect Woman

1

Both in the realm of philosophy and in mainstream society, the idea of the perfect woman has long been a topic of fascination and debate. Many theories about the characteristics of the perfect woman, and the question of whether such a woman actually exists, have advanced from classical Greece to modern civilization.

The 19th-century philosopher Arthur Schopenhauer is the source of one of the strangest theories about the perfect woman. Schopenhauer claimed that because women are inherently illogical, they are unable to attain true intellectual and moral greatness. However, he believed that there was one woman who was an exception to this rule, and that was the perfect woman.

Schopenhauer believed that the perfect woman was a rare and mythical creature who could rise beyond her inherent irrationality to reach a state of unadulterated morality and intellect. He felt that this woman would embody the ideal of feminine beauty and grace, as well as all the attributes of a decent person, such as compassion, selflessness, and wisdom.

This idea of the perfect woman is fundamentally problematic in addition to being bizarre. Schopenhauer's belief that women are illogical and subordinate to men stems from a long tradition of sexism and misogyny in Western philosophy. He perpetuates unattainable and destructive ideals for women to aspire to by idealizing femininity in ways that are nearly impossible to achieve.

Furthermore, the notion that women must restrain their inborn urges and emotions in order to succeed is not only constrictive but also invalidates women's experiences. It is hardly surprising that women sometimes defy conventional notions of logic and reason since we have historically been denied access to education and other opportunities for intellectual growth.

Our patriarchal society promotes the idea of the ideal woman. It is responsible for developing and upholding these unrealistic beauty standards that are, for the most part, out of reach for the majority of women. And to add more fuel to the flame, the media constantly bombards us with highly-edited images of flawless complexions and unnaturally perfect physiques that can be detrimental to the self-esteem of a young woman growing up in the 21st century.

It is worth mentioning that women of color, those with disabilities, and others who don't adhere to conventional gender norms are frequently excluded by the beauty myth because they don't conform to restrictive definitions of beauty. A lack of representation in the media and other cultural arenas can result from this, as well as sentiments of marginalization and exclusion.

Also, the notion that women must spend a lot of time on their looks in order to meet social expectations can be challenging, particularly for working mothers because they may have less time and money to invest in their appearance.

As a result, the idea of the perfect woman has led to an increase in plastic surgery, cosmetic operations, and eating disorders. It allows young women to put themselves under the knife or even risk their health to achieve this "ideal appearance." *The Beauty Myth* by Naomi Wolf is one book that shows the validity of this. In this book, Wolf points out that the pressure society places on people to adhere to a particular standard of beauty is the same pressure used to oppress and control women.

She claims that striving for physical perfection is not only unattainable but also problematic for women's emotional and physical health. Many examples from history and modern life support Wolf's claim. One that Wolf mentions is from the Victorian age when women were expected to have a tiny waist, a voluptuous body, and fair skin. Women were made to wear corsets to meet these expectations, which deformed their bodies and had adverse health effects. Women today are held to the same kind of unhealthy expectations, except now we have social media, celebrity culture, and the growing beauty industry to help spread and uphold this concept.

Wolf also states that the beauty myth distracts women from achieving true equality. Women are persuaded to spend time and money on beauty products and treatments because they are misinformed that their value is based on appearance. This prevents women from achieving their objectives and reaching their full potential.

Trivial matters of appearance can serve as a diversion from more significant concerns affecting women, such as gender inequality, reproductive rights, and job discrimination. Women who are preoccupied with their beauty may be less likely to participate in action and advocacy for these causes.

Furthermore, Wolf stresses that society as a whole

is harmed by the quest for the ideal woman and not just individual women. When half of the human population is not living up to its full potential, our society ultimately loses.

Additionally, the beauty myth perpetuates the idea that women are only appreciated for their appearance and not for their intelligence or accomplishments. This idea minimizes the complexity of women, making the assumption that all we have to worry about is looking pretty. This is definitely not the case for the majority of women throughout history.

Women have jobs and careers, goals and aspirations, and real problems and opinions that matter. We no longer have the time and energy to deal with unrealistic expectations forced on us by society.

Therefore, we must abandon this idea of the "perfect woman" and work towards embracing our own depth and personality that makes each of us unique. However, in order to let go of this concept, we must understand how we were made to think this way in the first place.

The Unfair Advantage

In her book *Brave, Not Perfect,* Reshma Saujani discusses how girls are taught from a young age to strive for perfection, as opposed to boys, who are encouraged to be brave and take risks. Reshma emphasizes that this disparity between how girls and boys are taught is damaging. She explains that it restricts girls from wanting to explore new interests, take chances, and achieve their aspirations in adolescence and as they grow into women.

Girls are often expected to put their appearance above all else. To be polite and compassionate, even if that means putting up with disrespect. To dress taste-fully for people to like you. Meanwhile, boys are less pressured to adhere to certain behaviors. Boys are taught that it's okay for them to be loud. It's okay for them to take risks, play around and be silly.

Society says, "boys will be boys," and their behaviors are consistently excused. They are praised as long as they're physically strong, good at sports, and don't show "girly" emotions. Although this concept of gender roles may seem to favor boys and give them an unfair advantage, being held to gender roles actually harms both genders. But that's a conversation for another day.

Furthermore, as we grow into women, this unfair

advantage continues to be established. In high school, girls must adhere to strict clothing policies so they don't "cause a distraction" for boys and male teachers on the premises. This fosters a culture where girls are forced to compromise their personal style and cover themselves up in order to satisfy the expectations of boys and men. Girls also face harsh judgment for being too forceful and confident. While boys are perceived as "bold" and "assertive," girls with the same attitude are perceived as "bossy" and "difficult."

Similarly, grown women who are driven and ambitious are condemned for being "too masculine" and "too focused on their professions." On the other hand, men who exhibit the same traits are commended for their commitment and work ethic.

Undoubtedly, this is one of many double standards that create an unfair advantage for boys and men alike. For this reason, women now have to put in extra work as adults in order to unlearn this deep-rooted belief that we have to choose between our ambition and our femininity.

The Marriage Plot

Throughout history, women have been under intense social pressure to get married and have kids. This expectation has resulted in a limited perception of what constitutes a successful relationship. One illustration of this is the marriage plot, a popular literary and cinematic device that portrays women's pursuit of marriage as their ultimate objective. However, women who are not interested in marriage or might not fit the stereotype of a wife and mother may suffer from this limited perspective.

For generations, authors have utilized the marriage plot as a literary device to portray tales of romance and relationships. It typically involves a young woman looking for a successful marriage, and the plot centers around her different suitors and romantic involvements. The underlying message of this, while seemingly innocent, is that a woman's value depends on her capacity to find a husband and establish a family. This limited perspective on relationships disregards the variety of human experiences and can be extremely harmful to those who do not match the standard pattern of a wife and mother.

The marriage plot's main flaw is that it perpetuates the notion that women are incomplete without a man. This damaging message can cause single women to suffer the effects of self-doubt and anxiety. It also reinforces the idea that women should place a higher value on romantic relationships than other facets of their lives, including their careers or friendships. This message can be particularly difficult for young women who are still developing their identities and trying to understand what they want from life.

The Good Girl Syndrome

Similar to the idea of the perfect woman, a cultural myth known as "the good girl syndrome" places unreasonably high demands on women to adhere to a specific code of conduct. Being respectful, well-mannered, and subservient are all part of this ideal, as well as adhering to gender norms. This expectation frequently causes women to internalize the idea that their value is based on their capacity to achieve these demands, which leads to low self-esteem and feeling inadequate.

In her book *Girl, Wash Your Face*, Rachel Hollis addresses this problem by discussing how she personally dealt with the good girl syndrome and how it impacted her self-esteem and personal development. Hollis writes about her struggles to live up to the standards set for her by her family and society, including being the ideal wife, mother, and housekeeper. Her remorse over being unable to meet these demands created a painful cycle of self-doubt and shame.

Hollis contends that the good girl syndrome, like the perfect woman ideology, is damaging to women because it is impossible to maintain without some sort of lasting cognitive dissonance. She stresses that women should be free to embrace their flaws and pursue their dreams without worrying about being criticized, or branded as "bad" or "unworthy." She also emphasizes the value of loving and caring for oneself to counteract the harmful impacts of the good girl syndrome.

By reaffirming traditional gender norms and limiting success for women, the good girl syndrome further contributes to gender inequality. Women are frequently discouraged from pursuing male-dominated industries or leadership roles because they are deemed too "emotional" or "illogical" to hold these types of positions.

Ultimately, the effects of the good girl syndrome have the potential to perpetuate the notion of the perfect wife by promoting a restricted view of femininity that values submission and self-sacrifice over individuality and self-expression.

In fact, the idea of the perfect wife has been a long-standing social construct that has been influenced by patriarchal customs and gender conventions. Women are traditionally expected to perform specific duties in the house and in their interactions with men. These expectations have put enormous pressure on women to live up to the romanticized idea of the ideal wife, which has had several unfavorable effects.

The idea that women exist solely to serve men is at the core of these social expectations. Because men have traditionally held positions of power and influence in economic, cultural, and religious organizations, this is believed to be true. Meanwhile women are consigned to the home, where they are expected to take care of the house and children as well as support their husbands' dreams and vocations.

Such societal expectations of the perfect wife can also negatively affect men. Men are often expected to be powerful, assertive, and dominant, which can create a sense of pressure to adhere to traditional gender norms. This pressure can lead to a lack of emotional feelings and intimacy in relationships, as men may feel that they cannot display vulnerability or weakness without being seen as less masculine.

The concept of the "perfect wife" often entails the expectation that women prioritize caregiving and put others' needs before their own. Women are expected to be unselfish and nurturing, whether in the form of child care, managing domestic duties, or supporting their partner's goals.

However, this expectation can be quite harmful and pressure women to compromise their well-being for others. It's critical to understand that being a good partner or caregiver does not entail putting one's own needs and preferences aside. Instead, it's about striking a balance and allocating equal importance to one's own needs as well as others'.

The Expectation to Prioritize Caregiving

The term "caregiver" describes the social and cultural expectation that we as women, especially mothers, are obligated to put caregiving for our kids, partner, and family ahead of other elements of our lives, such as our careers or personal aspirations.

This expectation is, once again, based on outdated gender roles. It reinforces the idea that it's a man's role to provide financially for the family while a woman's role is to be the caregiver and homemaker. As a result, women place their own goals and aspirations on hold so they can fulfill their expected duties.

At the same time, caregivers and homemakers are substantially undervalued in this capitalist society. Because these women, who provide free labor, are technically not earning an income from the services they provide, many people don't see the value of having a stay-at-home wife or mother. Therefore, their efforts in a role that was forced upon them are not appreciated.

The pervasive misconception is that taking care of family and household work is not a "real" job, even though providing familial care while running an entire household requires endless hours of effort and attention.

Additionally, husbands with stay-at-home wives benefit greatly from the personalized knowledge and planning required to run a household and take care of children. According to Care.com, employing a personal chef, reliable housekeeper, and trusted babysitter can cost an average of $62,400, $19,760, and $28,704 per year, respectively. Keep in mind that the value of these services may vary based on the cost of living in a particular area.

As you can see, stay-at-home mothers save their families a lot of money by taking on all these tasks themselves. The quantifiable contributions to their households are quite noticeable if you look at the bigger picture of what it takes to run a family.

Furthermore, research has shown that children raised by stay-at-home mothers have better emotional and social development than those who aren't. Thus, it's proven that stay-at-home moms are not just saving their families tons of money, but also creating a positive impact on the future of society.

Nonetheless, housework is continually undervalued in today's society because it's traditionally viewed as "women's work." This belief contributes to the gender pay gap because it reinforces the concept that women's labor is less valuable than men's and feeds prejudices about gender roles in the workforce.

The Gender Pay Gap

Another form of discrimination against women is the gender pay gap, an ongoing issue that began when women broke into the labor force. Despite the notable progress made toward gender equality in the past decades, the pay gap is still a persistent problem in many countries around the world.

The reasons for the gender pay gap are varied, and there is no single explanation for why it still exists. One factor is the persistent segregation of women into lower-paying professions and industries. Women are more likely to be employed in traditionally female-dominated occupations like teaching, nursing, and administrative support, while men are hired in higher-paying fields such as engineering, computer science, and finance. This occupational segregation is often driven by gender stereotypes and prejudices that restrict women's opportunities to pursue certain jobs.

The undervaluation of women's labor is another element that contributes to the gender pay gap. Tasks traditionally performed by women, such as childcare, cleaning, and personal care, are often underrated and underpaid in comparison to those of a similar nature performed by men. This undervaluation is partially caused by the perception that women's work is less significant or skillful, even when it entails high levels of responsibility and expertise.

The gender pay gap is a kind of discrimination that feeds into gender stereotypes and the notion that women are second-class employees, in addition to being a matter of economic inequality. It conveys to women that their labor is not as valuable as men's, and that they don't deserve equal pay for equal work.

A range of measures are required to eliminate the gender pay gap, including efforts to stop occupational segregation, advance equal compensation for equal work, and deal with the unequal distribution of unpaid care tasks. These initiatives should also address the underlying social and cultural practices that support traditional gender roles and restrict women's possibilities for professional success.

The Madonna-Whore Complex

The Madonna-Whore Complex is a double standard in which women can be one of two ways; clean and virtuous or promiscuous and immoral. While at the same time, men are applauded for having a long list of sexual partners. This type of thinking is firmly embedded in our culture and significantly impacts how women are viewed and treated.

The Madonna-Whore complex has its roots in a long history of patriarchal beliefs that treated women as things to be manipulated and exploited for men's pleasure. Those who are chaste and moral are considered the best candidates for marriage and motherhood, while those who engage in sexual activity outside of these parameters are ostracized and shamed.

This concept has a lot of adverse consequences for women. While "Madonnas" are required to uphold stringent standards of purity and modesty, women perceived as "whores" are often the targets of prejudice and abuse. Women are put in a position where they can't win because they will be negatively criticized regardless of their actions.

In addition, the complex fosters a culture in which it is unacceptable for women to express their sexuality and declare their personal preferences. Sexually active women are often shunned and alienated, which can make them feel ashamed and result in low self-esteem. This can have long-lasting impacts on a woman's mental health and well-being.

Men are often also affected by the Madonna-Whore complex. While women are held to certain expectations under this idea, there is also a significant amount of pressure put on men to adhere to the stereotypes that come with their gender. Under this belief, men are expected to have, and are praised for having, a long list of sexual partners. In contrast, those who aren't sexually active are considered weak and insufficient.

Recognizing and rejecting these damaging societal conventions is essential. Men should be encouraged to see women as complex people with a variety of interests and desires, and women should be free to explore their sexuality without worrying about prejudice.

Domestic Violence

Domestic violence, sometimes referred to as intimate partner violence, is a widespread issue that affects people and families all over the world. Studies show that women are more likely than men to face severe forms of abuse from their partners. These acts of violence might be physical, emotional, psychological, financial, or even sexual in nature. Due to patriarchal structures that put men's power and control above women's safety and well-being, women are typically expected to tolerate abuse and violence from partners or family members.

Many nations worldwide have a strong tradition of expecting women to put up with violence and abuse in their relationships. Cultural ideals that women should be subordinate to men usually serve as fuel for this. These ideas help to foster a culture of violence where men are urged to dominate and control women. Due to their fear of speaking up or getting help, women can end up being forced into remaining in abusive relationships or suffering in silence.

Domestic abuse may have catastrophic impacts on women, hurting their physical and mental health, capacity to work, and relationships with their kids. Domestically abused women are more prone to suffer from depression, anxiety, and other mental health illnesses. Also, they are more likely to sustain physical wounds including cuts, bruises, and broken bones. Domestic violence can even be fatal in extreme cases.

The social norm which upholds the view that women should endure abuse in their relationships is one of the most significant obstacles to ending domestic violence against women. If a woman speaks out against domestic abuse, she could be held responsible or even accused of inciting it. Because of this mindset, women find it challenging to leave abusive relationships or seek treatment, which promotes the cycle of violence.

We need to challenge the patriarchal systems that uphold the belief that women should tolerate abuse from their spouses to end this ideology. This entails advancing gender equality and giving women a voice so they can speak out against domestic abuse. It also involves supporting women who have been the victims of domestic violence and seeing to it that the perpetrators of abuse are held accountable for their crimes. Offering assistance and services to abused victims, such as secure housing, therapy, and legal representation is another step we can take towards preventing domestic abuse.

Accessing these resources might be difficult for many victims of domestic violence due to factors like financial instability or a lack of understanding of the available services. We can help victims of domestic violence recover and rebuild their lives by addressing these obstacles and offering our full support.

Breaking the Mold

Women have constantly been expected to conform to society's norms and regulations, whether it be the obligation to care for others or restrictions on their access to education and employment prospects. However, numerous women have overcome these assumptions and succeeded in professions that have been historically dominated by men. These trailblazers are proof of what is possible when women do not let cultural norms limit them.

Ruth Bader Ginsburg, a former Associate Justice of

the United States Supreme Court, is one example of a woman who challenged cultural norms. Throughout her career, Ginsburg overcame several challenges, including sexism and discrimination in the legal community. She fought against discrimination in areas like employment, housing, and education. She persisted and rose to prominence for her work promoting women's rights and gender equality. By breaking the gender barrier and becoming one of the first women to hold a position on the Supreme Court, Ginsburg inspired women all around the world.

Serena Williams is another woman who has excelled despite social expectations. Williams is regarded as one of the all-time greatest tennis players and has amassed 23 Grand Slam victories. She has prevailed in her sport and serves as an inspiration for female athletes all over the world despite having experienced prejudice and discrimination throughout her career. She has also used her position to speak out against racial inequality and police brutality to promote social justice.

There are countless other examples of successful women who have defied conventions, such as novelist Toni Morrison and astronaut Sally Ride. These women have inspired many to pursue their aspirations no matter what challenges they may encounter by demonstrating that it is possible to succeed despite society's expectations.

It is crucial to acknowledge the accomplishments made by these women in the past and encourage women who are breaking the mold today. Even though gender equality has progressed recently there is still much to be done, especially regarding pay fairness and representation in leadership roles. We can contribute to developing a more fair and just society by encouraging women who disregard societal expectations.

These women who have come before us have repeatedly shown that gender should never be a barrier to success. Their experiences serve as a reminder that with hard work, determination, and perseverance, you too can achieve your goals and leave a lasting impression on the world.

To start the journey of growth, we must realize that perfectionism is not necessary for success. In reality, unlearning perfectionism is actually the first step towards achieving your goals.

Part Two

The Five Steps to Personal Growth for Women in Their 20s

2

Step One: Unlearn Perfectionism

Perfectionism is a personality trait characterized by high levels of self-criticism, an ongoing quest for perfection, and a dread of making mistakes. Perfectionism can sometimes be a positive motivator, but it can also cause tension and anxiety, which can result in procrastination, self-doubt, and a sense that one is never good enough.

Instability within the family is one of the leading causes of perfectionism. Families who place a high value on exemplary academic and professional achievement tend to put a scarring amount of pressure on their children to perform well in every aspect of their lives. This can create a family culture that views perfectionism as a positive character trait, which can foster a mindset that is difficult to shake in adulthood.

Past successes or failures may be another source of perfectionism. For instance, you might have achieved a high degree of success in a certain area and now feel pressure to keep up that level of accomplishment, even though it is not sustainable. Or you might have encountered harsh criticism after falling short of a goal and now you feel the need to be flawless in order to avoid repeating the same experiences.

Unlearning perfectionism requires you to not only free yourself from the unrealistic expectations of your family and society, but also to let go of the damaging standards you set for yourself because of those expectations. In order to achieve this, you must accept that imperfection is a normal and essential part of the human experience. You'll need to change your perspective from one that is rigidly focused on success and failure to one that is more open-minded and compassionate toward your progress.

Recognizing perfectionism's harmful effects on your life is one of the first steps to unlearning it. The loop of always striving and never feeling content can leave you overwhelmed and might lead to burnout. Moreover, it may result in an overemphasis on seeking outward approval rather than internal motivation and personal satisfaction. Acknowledging these negative effects can help you understand the value of letting go of your perfectionistic drives.

Furthermore, perfectionism has practical drawbacks in addition to emotional ones. Perfectionism can cause you to procrastinate on a task because you are unsure that you can complete it perfectly. As a result, you waste valuable time getting every little detail right before actually starting anything. This paradox, known as perfection paralysis, prevents you from moving forward and hinders your growth.

Be prepared to question your ideas of success and develop a mindset more oriented toward growth. It's helpful to see your mistakes as a direction in which you need to learn and grow rather than being focused on outcomes and results. Keep in mind that unlearning perfectionism takes time, effort, and self-reflection. Adopting a forgiving attitude toward yourself takes practice and persistence.

"You and only you are ultimately responsible for who you become and how happy you are"

— *Rachel Hollis, 2018*

In this quote, best-selling author Rachel Hollis

points out that happiness and identity are ultimately up to us. Even if our prior experiences affected who we are today, it's up to us to break the cycle of suffering and create the life we desire. We can do this by taking responsibility for our own growth and happiness instead of letting our past circumstances get the best of us.

It's easy to fall into the trap of blaming other people and things for your own issues and unhappiness. It's valid to feel you've been dealt a bad hand or weren't given the right opportunities but staying in that mindset is unproductive and only impedes your progress. In essence, you are in control of your life. Accepting that you have the power to change your own life frees you from feeling stuck in a situation you can't control. You can either let your past define who you are or decide to write a new story about yourself.

At the end of the day, finding happiness and bettering yourself is a personalized path where only you can make the decisions. To build the life you want, you have to look deep into yourself and make the necessary adjustments to your mindset that are limiting you from living a fulfilling life.

Here are nine essential ideas to help you adjust your mindset and make progress toward unlearning perfectionism.

Embrace Your Imperfections

Brené Brown, the author of *The Gifts of Imperfection: Let Go of Who You Think You're Supposed to Be and Love Who You Are*, gives her readers the motivation to embrace imperfection and emphasize the process over the result. Brown contends that striving for perfection is counter-productive because true pleasure and happiness come from being vulnerable and authentic to oneself.

Embracing your imperfections involves giving yourself the grace to learn and grow from your mistakes while loving every imperfect part of yourself that you cannot change. Emphasis on the learn and grow part, because learning and growing requires you to take accountability for your actions and dig deep into why you act and react a certain way.

It also involves letting go of the need for approval from others and recognizing that your value is not based on your physical appearance or ability to meet societal standards. You are valuable just for being who you are because your value comes from within.

In fact, your flaws give your personality depth and character. They may even be the reason people adore you. You're doing yourself a disservice by trying to conceal your flaws or act as if they don't exist.

Practice Vulnerability

Vulnerability is being frank and open about your feelings, opinions, and experiences. It is essential for creating lasting connections and promoting personal development. Brené Brown's book *Daring Greatly: How the Courage to Be Vulnerable Transforms the Way We Live, Love, Parent, and Lead* explains that while practicing vulnerability can be difficult, it can also have enormous advantages.

According to Brown's reasoning in *Daring Greatly*, vulnerability is not a sign of weakness but rather the starting point of creativity and human connection. She argues that vulnerability requires courage, empathy, and willingness to accept risks. Developing stronger relationships with people is one of the main advantages of vulnerability. In intimate relationships, it can strongly impact emotional intimacy and bonding between partners because you open the door to empathy and compassion when you let people see the real you. Practicing vulnerability can lead to a life filled with more joy, harmony, and purpose.

The ability to overcome guilt and self-doubt is another advantage of vulnerability. Shame flourishes in secrecy and silence, and vulnerability can help you escape the cycle of shame by enabling you to be honest about your flaws and difficulties. You can learn to accept yourself fully and grow in your ability to be compassionate toward yourself by accepting vulnerability.

Vulnerability can also serve as a springboard for creativity and personal development. When you are willing to take chances and accept uncertainty, you can discover and innovate by opening up to new thoughts and experiences. Entrepreneurs and leaders who wish to foster creativity and effect positive change must be vulnerable.

Of course, cultivating vulnerability may be difficult, especially in a culture that frequently prioritizes self-reliance and strength over openness and connection. The risks and uncertainties that come with vulnerability can be challenging to manage and require courage and resilience. Nevertheless, those who are willing to take the plunge can undergo significant personal growth and transformation since the benefits of vulnerability far outweigh the risks.

You have to understand that living in a society that prizes invulnerability and excellence inhibits us from being vulnerable. Social standards force us to hide our flaws and inadequacies in order to project a pristine picture to the outside world. This attitude toward life is ultimately unsustainable and can lead to isolation and detachment. Therefore, you should be able to accept the discomfort of being vulnerable and be receptive to criticism and support from others.

Accept Your Failures and Mistakes

Being able to accept your failures and mistakes comes alongside being vulnerable. A meaningful existence requires you to love yourself despite the errors you've made in the past.

For you to improve yourself and succeed in life, you must learn to acknowledge your setbacks. Although it may seem contradictory, accepting your mistakes can be an effective way to learn from them. It's not only important to accept your mistakes but to make them too. In fact, it's crucial to make mistakes in order to learn significant lessons in life, like dating the wrong person, failing a test, or saying the wrong thing at an interview. Mistakes guide you in the right direction. *Mindset: The New Psychology of Achievement* by Carol Dweck is one book that offers evidence of the validity and advantages of embracing mistakes and failure.

There are two kinds of mindsets that the author discusses; the fixed mindset and the growth mindset. People with a fixed mindset believe their skills and talents are unchangeable traits. Some may find it difficult to take chances or attempt new things because they see errors and failures as reflections of their inherent limits. On the other hand, those who have a growth mindset think their skills and traits can be improved with commitment and effort. People with a growth mindset are more likely to take on challenges and persevere despite setbacks because they view mistakes and failures as chances to learn and progress.

Research provides ample evidence that adopting a growth mindset can increase success and happiness in life. For instance, research done with a group of seventh graders indicated that those who were taught a growth mindset were more likely to embrace challenges and obtain higher grades than those taught a fixed mindset. Also, athletes with a growth mentality were more resilient in the face of failure and willing to keep working out and getting better.

One of the main advantages of accepting mistakes and failures is that it gives you more confidence to take risks and pursue your objectives. You are more open to face challenges that may initially seem intimidating when you perceive mistakes and failures as chances for improvement. You understand that setbacks and failures are a normal part of learning and that each failure moves you one step closer to success. This can be especially useful in professional settings, where taking calculated chances and accepting new challenges can lead to professional growth and greater job satisfaction.

Furthermore, accepting mistakes and failure can boost resilience and mental stability. You gain more self-confidence in your abilities after each obstacle you conquer and failure you recover from. The ability to manage challenging situations and emerge stronger on the other side can be especially beneficial during stressful and uncertain times.

Practice Self-Compassion

Another key practice to remember when unlearning perfectionism is self-compassion. Self-compassion is the practice of treating yourself with the same consideration, kindness, and understanding that you would extend to a close friend or family member. It's the capacity to forgive mistakes, like being a few minutes late for dinner or forgetting to wash your dirty dishes in the sink after a long day of work. Being able to forgive yourself will make accepting your mistakes and learning from them easier as well. In fact, cultivating self-compassion has many positive effects on our mental health, interpersonal connections, and general well-being.

According to Kristin Neff and Christopher Germer in their book *The Mindful Self-Compassion Workbook*, there are three key elements of self-compassion: self-kindness, common humanity, and mindfulness.

Self-kindness calls for you to treat yourself with love, understanding, and forgiveness. Common humanity is the understanding that everyone experiences sadness and that you are not alone in the challenges you face. The last key element is practicing mindfulness, which involves being present and conscious of your thoughts and feelings without allowing them to control you.

For example, they mention a study which shows that cultivating self-compassion might enhance your mental health. The study revealed that people who were taught self-compassion had much lower levels of anxiety and depression than those who were not. The authors also mention the connection between self-compassion and resilience, which showed that those who exhibit greater self-compassion are better equipped to recover from failures and deal with challenging circumstances.

Apart from improving your mental health, practicing self-compassion can also enhance your relationships. When you are more self-compassionate, you can establish deeper connections with others and offer them compassion as well. This is due to the fact that when you are not condemning or criticizing yourself, you are less prone to criticize others. Research shows that more self-compassionate people are more inclined to forgive others and feel closer to their friends and family.

Self-compassion can also improve your physical health. The body's inflammation, which is linked to several health issues like heart disease, diabetes, and cancer, is lower in people who practice self-compassion. Studies have also demonstrated that practicing self-compassion enhances immunological performance and lessens the damaging effects of stress on the body.

A simple and effective way to dial in self-compassion is to use daily affirmations to remind yourself that you deserve love and compassion. You could even try writing a letter to yourself from the viewpoint of a compassionate friend or giving yourself a big hug. Implementing these things into your daily routine can enhance your relationships as well as your physical and mental health.

Set Achievable Objectives

Setting realistic objectives is a key element of success in any aspect of life. This is particularly true when it comes to personal and professional progress. Establishing a clear and achievable set of goals can help guide your actions and focus your efforts on achieving your desired results. While it may be tempting to set lofty and ambitious goals, research has shown that realistic objectives often foster motivation and increase performance over the long haul.

It's crucial to set realistic expectations that are achievable and aligned with your values and priorities. I have found that this is especially pertinent for women who often face societal pressure to juggle multiple roles and excel in every aspect of their lives.

When establishing practical goals, it's wise to take a step back and review your current situation. Ask yourself: What are my strengths and weaknesses?; what are my immediate and future priorities?; and what are my resources? If you have the answers to these questions, setting proper goals will be easier for you.

The Art of Possibility by Rosamund Stone Zander and Benjamin Zander is one book that offers evidence of the advantages of having realistic goals. In this book, the authors argue that having realistic goals fosters a higher sense of creativity and possibility in addition to being more practical and doable. The authors advise establishing more general goals that permit flexibility and experimentation rather than limiting oneself to overly detailed ones.

One of the main advantages of setting realistic goals is the ability to foster a sense of self-efficacy and confidence. When you create realistic objectives and are able to achieve them, it increases your sense of self-worth and develops your belief in your own skills. For instance, if your family is your first priority, then aiming to spend more time with your family is likely to be more important and attainable than a goal to work 80 hours per week .

When minor goals are accomplished, it can generate a positive feedback loop where motivation and confidence are increased for tackling future, more difficult and larger tasks. When setting targets, it's also essential to monitor your progress regularly. This boosts your motivation and enables you to change your targets as necessary.

For example, if you set a goal to exercise three times a week but find it difficult to maintain such a schedule, you may need to adjust your goal to two times a week. Regularly monitoring your progress also helps you determine your achievements and pinpoint areas that require development.

Additionally, you can prioritize your work more effectively and devote your attention to accomplishing your goals when you are clear on what you want to achieve. Breaking down large goals into smaller, more achievable steps can help reduce tension and overload.

This can support your ability to recover from setbacks and continue with your ambitions. Establishing reasonable goals might encourage increased innovation and creativity. You may be more receptive to investigating other scenarios and trying out novel strategies when you are not unduly fixated on particular results. This can lead to unanticipated discoveries and solutions that might not have been feasible if you were exclusively focused on reaching a specific goal.

Furthermore, establishing reasonable goals can help you become more resilient and persistent in the face of difficulties. Having a specific goal to work toward when you face challenges might help you stay motivated and concentrate on finding solutions.

Learn to Say No

If you have people-pleasing tendencies, as most women do, it might be difficult for you to refuse a request, whether it's reasonable or not. The idea that we should be accommodating and prioritize the needs of others over our own has long been ingrained into us by society. However, saying yes to everything no matter what it costs us leads to exhaustion and burnout. Thus, learning to say no is essential.

In today's society, women have gained independence and made progress toward equality by joining the workforce and earning financial freedom. As a consequence, societal standards have shifted from the perfect woman and the good girl syndrome, in which women were expected to fit an ideal appearance and conform to gender roles in their relationships and household, to now perpetuating the image of the "superwoman." The superwoman myth holds the idea that women are able to effortlessly balance their education, careers, families, and personal well-being all by themselves.

Despite the many difficulties and impediments that each of these areas presents, women are often expected to juggle and excel at all of these tasks without so much as a complaint. However, the pressure to maintain constant excellence in all aspects of their lives often results in a decline in a woman's mental and physical health.

Even though saying "no" is often seen as selfish and self-centered, it is necessary because it enables us to prioritize our own needs and set healthy boundaries with the people in our lives. Learning to say no means accepting that we have limitations; we can only help people if we take care of ourselves first. Understanding that we cannot provide our best if we are overworked and neglecting our well-being is important.

The ability to refuse a request can also be empowering. It enables us to take charge of our lives and make decisions about our own desires and requirements. Instead of just responding to other people's expectations, it allows us to concentrate on the things that are most important to us.

Keep in mind that setting boundaries does not require impoliteness or confrontation. There are appropriate and courteous ways to say no to a request.

Saying, "Thank you for thinking of me, but I am unable to commit to that right now," is a polite way to turn down an invitation.

Setting boundaries also makes it clear who actually respects you and who doesn't. There will be instances when you decline a request and someone refuses to take no for an answer. Take note of who these people are, as people who disregard your boundaries don't respect you as a person.

Developing the ability to set clear boundaries calls for self-awareness and self-compassion. Knowing when you are stretched too thin and need to put your health first is imperative.

Seek Help

We all experience times in life when we need help. Asking for assistance can be difficult, particularly when we feel exposed or fear being judged. But getting help has many advantages that can boost our physical and emotional health. In *The Art of Asking*, Amanda Palmer discusses the value of asking for help and how it can improve our lives.

Palmer stresses that asking for help is not a show of weakness, but rather a sign of power. It might be challenging to ask for assistance, but it can also be a chance for connection and progress. Asking for help can be intimidating because we worry it will make us seem weak or unprepared. Palmer contends, however, that when we reach out for assistance, we put ourselves in a position to potentially gain helpful advice, resources, and support from others.

One of the key benefits of seeking help is that it can alleviate stress and anxiety. When you are struggling with a problem or issue, it can be overwhelming to try to solve it on your own. Seeking help from friends, family, or professionals can provide you with relief and reassurance that you are not alone. This, in turn, can reduce your stress levels and promote better mental health.

Seeking help might also help you build stronger relationships with others. By requesting help, you open the door for others to interact with you and learn from your experiences. As a result, you may feel a sense of community and belonging, which is crucial for your mental health. Due to your increased awareness of other people's struggles, asking for assistance can also help develop empathy and compassion for others.

Seeking a trusted mentor is also important in personal or professional situations. Having a mentor who is knowledgeable about your desired subject can be really helpful because of the direction and advice they can provide. By taking advantage of the fresh perspective, advice, and insights a mentor can offer, you can improve dramatically in your personal and professional career.

I struggled to ask for help for a long time because I was in my masculine energy of wanting to do everything myself. However, as I learned to lean into my feminine energy, which we will discuss later in the book, I was able to let go of this belief and seek support from family, friends, and eventually a mentor. Only then was I able to make progress toward reaching my full potential and greater success in my career and personal life. This is because getting help gave me access to resources, information, and viewpoints I might not have had previously.

"Asking for help with shame says: 'You have the power over me.' Asking with condescension says: 'I have the power over you.' But asking for help with gratitude says: 'We have the power to help each other.'"

— *Amanda Palmer, 2019*

Focus On Progress, Not Perfection

Rather than striving for a perfect final product, emphasizing your progress enables you to put more significance on the process of learning and growing. This way of thinking has several benefits, both personally and professionally.

One of the main benefits of focusing on progress is that it lessens the pressure and stress brought on by the pursuit of perfection. Expecting yourself to perform at peak capacity at all times can result in anxiety and exhaustion. Concentrating on development is the more self-compassionate approach. It is incredibly valuable to realize that there will be times when you can only perform at 50 percent and that that is enough.

Focusing on progress also fosters a growth mindset, which is what we strive for. Instead of solely focusing on natural aptitude or abilities, it encourages a desire to learn and grow. As we discussed before, this mindset promotes resilience, flexibility, and creativity.

Setting goals can be done with more freedom when progress is the focus. Instead of aiming for the rigid definition of perfection, you can set goals that promote improvement while also being practical and attainable. As a result, you may feel more accomplished and satisfied because you can see actual progress being made.

Furthermore, instead of continually feeling inadequate due to the nature of the quest for perfection, concentrating on progress enables you to recognize and celebrate your accomplishments. You might experience a sense of pride in your work by recognizing the advancements you have made toward your goal. This could result in more drive and a desire to keep learning and developing.

Experience Gratitude And Joy

All of these important ideas in unlearning perfectionism boil down to one essential life goal; to improve your mental well-being. This, in turn, will help you experience gratitude and joy throughout your lifetime. Conveniently, the same concept applies vice versa; learning to feel gratitude and joy can change your life and improve your general well-being and happiness. By appreciating what you already have and all the things the universe graciously gave you, you can change your perceptions and discover meaning and purpose in your daily life. The book *The How of Happiness: A Scientific Approach to Getting the Life You Want* by Sonja Lyubomirsky explains the process of developing gratitude and joy.

In *The How of Happiness,* Lyubomirsky argues that happiness is not solely determined by external factors like wealth or status, but rather by how we think and behave. She stresses that cultivating happiness is a talent that can be taught by conscious effort. Being able to express happy emotions like joy and gratitude is one of the major things that contribute to happiness.

When you consider your accomplishments, think about what you've learned and what you've improved. Asking yourself questions such as: What difficulties did I resolve?; what new abilities did I gain?; which revelations did I make?; can help you better understand your accomplishments and the priceless experiences you've had.

Be happy about all kinds of accomplishments, no matter how big or small they may seem. You might have finished an assignment, found a new job, or met a personal objective. Recognizing little victories is just as important as the big ones: Did you wake up early this morning?; did you complete everything on your daily to-do list?; did you do a quick workout today? All of these accomplishments are worthy of appreciation.

Gratitude is a powerful emotion that people can develop with practice. Recognizing and appreciating the positive aspects of your life, such as your relationships, health, and opportunities, is a key component of gratitude. Reaching out to the people you love, keeping a gratitude journal, or simply pausing to think about your blessings are all methods of practicing thankfulness.

Savoring positive experiences by fully engaging in them, focusing on the present moment, and paying attention to the details increases joy and happiness. You can prolong and intensify the positive emotions associated with your unique experiences when you savor the moment.

In addition, doing more of the activities you enjoy will enhance happy feelings and boost overall health. Simple pleasures like reading a book, spending time with loved ones, or partaking in a hobby can add up to a fulfilling life.

It is crucial to cultivate positive relationships with others. Having strong social connections can enhance your happiness and well-being. By nurturing your relationships, you can experience a sense of belonging and social support, which can help you in times of difficulty and failure.

<hr />

PERFECTIONISM IS NOT AN INTRINSIC TRAIT. It's a taught behavior that can be unlearned with time, effort, and desire to change. This means that people who struggle with perfectionism are not inherently bad or broken, they have simply evolved a way of thinking that can be altered by working on bettering themselves.

Coming to terms with perfectionism can be challenging since you may have identified with it for a long time and seen it as an essential part of who you are. However, realizing that perfectionism is a learned trait can be freeing because it signifies a part of your identity that you can now change.

With this realization comes the inspiration to learn more about detachment, which involves letting go of your current or old identity and the need to control outcomes in your life.

3

Step Two: Detach Yourself From Your Old Identity

L etting go of your attachment to events, people, or identities can be difficult, but it can also be very liberating. Humans have a propensity for attachment that can, at times, be painful. When we become emotionally invested in anything, we base our pleasure and well-being on uncontrollable outside forces and set unrealistic expectations. In contrast, when we learn to be detached, we let go of expectations and desires and allow ourselves to be who we are, experiencing life as it unfolds.

The freedom to be ourselves is one of the main advantages of being unattached. Being authentic and true to ourselves is possible when we are not preoccupied with trying to influence or control the outcomes. When we don't feel concerned with other people's approval or living up to their expectations, it allows us to explore our own hobbies and passions. This kind of freedom is crucial for our own growth and development.

Being detached also enables us to live in the present moment by not trying to continually anticipate the future all the time. To develop mindfulness and cultivate inner peace, one must have this kind of presence.

Moreover, we must come to the understanding that attachment never serves us. When we are emotionally attached to something or someone, we are continuously looking for outside approval and acceptance. We start to depend on other people and things for our pleasure and well-being, which can result in negative emotions like tension, anxiety, and disappointment. In addition, when things don't go as planned, we can feel a great sense of loss and melancholy, as if a piece of ourselves has been taken away.

Being detached from people or things doesn't imply that we have no passion for them, it only means that we aren't reliant on them for our happiness and well-being. We can still have goals and dreams as long as we approach them with a sense of detachment from the outcome. We still have the ability to love and care for people, but we do it without expecting anything in return.

Here are ten strategies on how to live a life free of attachments.

Practice Self-Awareness

Self-awareness is the skill of objectively monitoring our own thoughts, emotions, and behaviors. We can use this skill to identify behavioral patterns that might not be beneficial to us and change them for the better. The development of self-awareness can also assist us in identifying our emotional attachments to particular people, things, or results. *The Power of Awareness* by Neville Goddard is a book that talks more about self-awareness and the power of the mind.

According to Neville Goddard, our beliefs and thoughts shape our personal reality. He contends that by increasing awareness of our thoughts, we can begin to shape our reality into the life we desire.

Goddard makes the point that we are not helpless victims of our surroundings. Instead, we have the ability to control our reality through our thoughts and beliefs. This means that we have the capacity to let go of our limiting ideas and thinking patterns and replace them with empowering, uplifting ones.

To do this you must be able to honestly and objectively examine yourself. Doing this will require you to identify your weaknesses as well as your strengths. However, once you make the practice of self-awareness a habit you will be able to single out specific people or instances that trigger something in you and respond more consciously and deliberately.

For example, a person who is attached to the outcome of getting straight A's in college may just be someone who desires to get a profitable job or internship after graduation. They might do anything and everything to get A's in their classes, not knowing that jobs and internships are actually not looking at grades or GPA when interviewing a potential job candidate.

If this person were to take a step back and become aware of why they're so attached to the outcome of getting a 4.0 GPA, they might realize that getting straight A's doesn't actually matter to them and that spending time prepping for interviews is what really matters. The ability to be self-aware benefits you greatly in letting go of your attachments. When you are able to identify the root cause of your attachment by being aware of your patterns and behaviors, it makes reaching your true goal that much easier.

Practice Mindfulness

The practice of mindfulness means being fully present in the moment and accepting all of your thoughts, feelings, and physical sensations without passing judgment. It's about living in the present and letting go of the past and the future. This straightforward technique can aid in lowering stress, boosting concentration, and enhancing general well-being.

The practice of mindfulness has Buddhist origins and has grown in popularity recently, primarily in the psychology field. According to research, mindfulness can lessen the signs of anxiety, despair, and chronic pain. Moreover, it has been shown to boost emotional control, enhance cognitive performance, and increase empathy and compassion for others (Mayo Clinic, n.d.).

Similar to the practice of self-awareness, practicing mindfulness plays a huge part in helping us let go of our attachments. By noticing our thoughts and feelings and accepting them without judgment, we can begin to recognize our thoughts and feelings for what they are —brief states of mind that will eventually dissipate. This plays into releasing our attachments because as you practice noting feelings as they arise and letting them go, you will also be able to let go of the feelings of comfort that come with certain attachments.

The Power of Now by Eckhart Tolle is a book that focuses on the value of being completely present in the moment and letting go of attachment to the past and future. Tolle suggests that most of our pain comes from our attachment to our thoughts and emotions. Sometimes, we get caught up in our own stories about the world and become disengaged from the reality of the present moment.

By practicing mindfulness, we can learn to give up these attachments and experience life as it is, in the present moment. We can discover a sense of peace and contentment when we shift our focus from the past and the future.

Tolle also believes that the only moment in which we have the power to act, alter our course, and build a better future for everyone is the one we are in right now. This idea suggests that the only moment we have the power to control is the present one. Therefore, we should savor every single moment we have; this, in turn, will allow us to continually experience gratitude and joy into the future.

It's important to note that our thoughts and feelings are not who we are. Rather, we constitute their awareness. By simply observing our thoughts and feelings without attachment or judgment to them, we can start to understand that they are just temporary mental states that do not define who we are.

When we allow a thought or feeling to overcome us, that is when we let it define who we are. For example, think of a time when someone did something to make you mad. You may have felt mad for a few moments and then let go of the feeling. But what if you were to continually hold on to that anger by playing the moment back over and over in your head for hours on end? That would probably cause you to be in a bad mood for hours. And if you held that feeling in for days, weeks, or months, it would foster a bad attitude and even a bitter personality. For this reason, practicing mindfulness is crucial for a happier, more fulfilling life.

Identify the Attachment

Our lives are shaped by the strong force of attachment in both subtle and profound ways. Our attachments are essential to our sense of identity and well-being, from the things we surround ourselves with to the people we value. But while attachment can bring quite a lot of happiness and fulfillment, it can also result in hurt, disappointment, and even misery. It is critical to be able to identify what our attachments are, understand why they matter to us, and how this affects our lives.

Our emotional connection to something, or someone, is at the heart of attachment. From a favorite childhood toy to a lifelong companion, this connection can take many different forms. What these attachments have in common is the sense of security, comfort, and belonging they provide. When we feel connected to something or someone, we experience a sense of security and continuity in our lives, as well as a sense of belonging to something bigger than ourselves.

Understanding who we are and how we interact with the world around us begins with identifying our attachments. Our attachments can disclose our priorities, values, and ambitions, as well as our worries, concerns, and insecurities. If a person is emotionally invested in their job, for instance, it might be because they place a high value on job success or financial stability. If someone is quick to become emotionally attached to another person, they may just crave intimacy, connection, and emotional support. We can learn more about our underlying motivations and ambitions by looking at our attachments.

Furthermore, it's crucial to understand that our attachments can also be a cause of pain. Too much attachment to something or someone might cause us to depend on it for our sense of well-being. We may feel a sense of loss, grief, or even depression if that bond is jeopardized or lost. For example, if a person is overly dependent on another person, they might experience stress and anxiety if they feel as if they're not living up to the other person's expectations or constantly doing something to make the other person happy. Being overly attached to someone might also cause us to be overbearing, possessive, or controlling, which can put a strain on the relationship.

It's imperative to acknowledge our attachments in order to mitigate their detrimental impacts. To achieve this, we must be able to recognize when we rely too heavily on someone or something. This will require you to practice self-awareness and mindfulness as we discussed previously.

Let Go of Expectations

We all deal with expectations on a daily basis. We have expectations for ourselves, other people, and our surroundings. These expectations can inspire and moti-vate us, pushing us to accomplish more than we previously believed was possible. But when we become obsessed with a specific result and grow attached to these expectations, disappointment and frustration are bound to happen when things don't go as planned. And rarely do they ever. In his book, *The Four Agreements*, Don Miguel Ruiz emphasizes the value of letting go of expectations in order to lead a happier, fulfilling life.

Holding onto expectations is simply attempting to control the future, which you may have realized is impossible. Many factors in life are unpredictable and beyond our control. Trying to control everything will ultimately lead to feelings of frustration. We run the risk of adopting a pessimistic mindset when we do this.

Expectations get in the way of being totally present in the moment and appreciating all that life has to offer. Instead of focusing just on the outcome, we can discover joy in the process of the pursuit of our goals. If we were solely concerned with a particular result, we might miss out on valuable lessons and experiences.

Letting go of your expectations does not mean you have to give up your goals and aspirations. It simply means that we should be open to whatever happens and understand that there's a bigger picture in play. This idea can cultivate a fearlessness of failure and a stronger sense of personal development as one builds the habit of letting go of their expectations.

Additionally, letting go of expectations can enhance our interactions with other people. When we hold people to expectations we are essentially attempting to control their behavior. Although it is reasonable to expect people to treat you fairly and with common decency, holding people to high expectations can cause conflict and misunderstanding. Instead of attempting to change someone, we can either accept them for who they are or remove them from our lives. In the long run, this will save space for people who add value to your life.

Embrace Impermanence

Our thoughts, emotions, and material items are all impermanent, transient and subject to change. Some people may find this truth difficult since they naturally cling to things that make them feel safe and comfortable. But by accepting impermanence, we can discover how to let go of attachment to fleeting things and find serenity in the now.

Many spiritual and philosophical traditions have long debated the idea of impermanence. Taoism is one such tradition that places a strong emphasis on living in harmony with the universe and acknowledging the transience of all things. Lao Tzu's famous work on Taoism, *The Tao Te Ching*, provides insight into the advantages of accepting impermanence.

Everything in life is transitory, including our thoughts, feelings, and material possessions. We can start to let go of attachment and find peace in the now by accepting this fact. It is crucial to live in harmony with the universe, which is always evolving. We can learn to flow with life's changes and find peace in the here and now by accepting impermanence and letting go of attachment.

Accepting impermanence can also assist us in getting through difficult times. We always feel loss and disappointment when things that are fleeting change or vanish, therefore it's best not to cling to them. We can lessen our suffering and achieve calm in the here and now by letting go of attachment and recognizing the transience of everything.

Accepting impermanence not only helps us experience less suffering but also makes life more satisfying. When we release our attachment to things that are temporary, we can concentrate our efforts on the things that really matter.

Focus on What You Can Control

Our propensity to become attached to things that are out of our control is one of the biggest challenges we encounter in life. We frequently find ourselves fixated on the outcome, whether it be a professional environment, a relationship, or a personal objective, even when there is nothing we can do to change it. Stress, anxiety, and even despair can result from this attachment to outcomes, which can be quite taxing.

It's crucial to concentrate on what we can manage in order to avoid falling into this trap. We can release ourselves from the worry and anxiety that are frequently associated with outcomes and situations by letting go of our attachment to them. This means focusing our attention on the things we can control and letting go of everything else.

Stephen Covey's *The 7 Habits of Highly Effective People* is one book that discusses this idea. The author's message in this book is to take ownership of our life and concentrate on the things we can alter rather than fret over the things that are out of our control. By doing this, we can feel more in control of our lives and take meaningful action to make those changes.

Covey talks about the value of concentrating on our sphere of influence. The elements in this circle that we have control over are things like our ideas, actions, and behaviors. By concentrating on this circle, we can focus our attention on the things that truly matter and let go of the things which are out of our control.

Proactive thinking is another significant habit mentioned by Covey. This is accepting accountability for our actions and realizing that we have the ability to decide how to react in various circumstances. We can take a proactive stance and decide to concentrate on the things that are within our control rather than simply responding to outside stimuli.

Shift Your Perspective

It's difficult to let go of attachment, but shifting your perspective and approaching the subject from a fresh angle might be helpful. We frequently become enmeshed in our own feelings and experiences to the point that we are unable to perceive the wider picture. We develop attachments to particular results or methods of operation, which can cause disappointment, annoyance, and even rage. But if we can change our viewpoint and approach the matter from a different angle, we might be able to let go of attachment and discover calm and acceptance.

Asking yourself some questions is one method to change your perspective. What would happen, for instance, if you let go of your attachment to this circumstance? Or asked yourself *What else can I do?* These questions can help you approach the issue from a fresh angle and identify the best strategy for achieving your desired outcome.

Putting yourself in someone else's shoes is another way of changing your opinion. Consider the problem from their perspective and endeavor to comprehend any potential motivations behind their feelings. This can assist you in letting go of your own attachment and gaining a more objective perspective. Consider trying to understand a friend's or family member's point of view if you and they are at odds. What apprehensions and worries do they have? What are their guiding principles and beliefs? By doing this, you might be able to discover some points of agreement and reach a compromise.

Sometimes you have to let go of your ego in order to change your perspective. Since we become so concerned with being right or winning an argument, our ego frequently prevents us from seeing things objectively. We might be able to let go of our attachment and arrive at a more amicable conclusion, though, if we can put aside our ego and approach things with humility and openness. Although doing so could necessitate an admission of guilt or an apology, it can also foster more empathy and better interpersonal ties.

Practicing gratitude is another approach to changing your perspective. When we concentrate on what we have to be thankful for, we may begin to see the bigger picture and value the positive aspects of our lives. This can assist us in letting go of our attachment to things that don't matter as much and putting our attention on the things that do in fact make us happy and fulfilled. For instance, if you're feeling frustrated about your job, try to concentrate on the parts for which you are glad, such as your coworkers or the chances for professional development.

The ability to change your perspective ultimately depends on your openness and willingness to consider new possibilities. At first, it could feel strange, but it can also feel freeing and empowering. You can discover acceptance and tranquility even in trying circumstances by letting go of attachment and adopting a different perspective. This can free you from the limitations of attachment and negativity, allowing you to live a more fulfilled and joyous life. Hence, the next time you feel stuck or frustrated, attempt to change your perspective and look at the situation from a fresh angle. The results could surprise you.

Engage in Physical Activity

Exercise can be a powerful tool to aid people in letting go of negative emotions and focusing on the present. It can be difficult to let go of unpleasant feelings like anger, grief, or fear. A healthy method to let these feelings out and direct them in a constructive direction is through physical activity. Exercise causes the body's natural feel-good chemicals, endorphins, to be released. Endorphins can increase emotions of happiness and well-being while also assisting in the reduction of pain and stress.

Exercise helps to lower the levels of stress chemicals like cortisol and adrenaline in the body in addition to releasing endorphins. These chemicals, which are secreted in reaction to stress, can cause tense and anxious feelings. We can help to lower the levels of these stress hormones by getting physical activity, which can help to reduce tension and promote relaxation.

A brisk walk or a more rigorous workout are both examples of physical activity. The secret is to choose a hobby that you take pleasure in and that complements your way of life. Getting in shape can be a terrific way to meet new people and interact, whether it be through sports teams or group fitness courses. For people who struggle with feelings of loneliness or isolation, the social aspect of exercise can be hugely helpful.

Exercise not only improves a person's physical and mental health, but it can also help let go of attachment to limiting beliefs and negative self-talk. Physical activity often forces us to face our own limits and pushes us to do things we may not have imagined were possible. In the long run, this can help to build confidence and self-esteem.

Limit Time Spent on Social Media or Digital Devices

In recent years, social media and digital devices have mostly taken over our daily lives. While there are many advantages to modern devices, such as the opportunity to interact with others and access a wealth of information, they can also be detrimental to our physical and mental health. Limiting time spent on social media or other digital devices has therefore gained popularity as a method of detachment.

Improving mental health is among the major perks of setting time limits for using social media and other digital devices. Excessive social media use has been linked in studies to emotions of despair, anxiety, and loneliness. We may compare ourselves to others on social media and feel inferior or alone. Reducing our time on social platforms can help us focus on our own lives and cut down on the time we spend comparing ourselves to others.

Reducing time spent on digital gadgets and social media can also improve physical health. Many of us spend a sizable chunk of the day staring at screens, whether it be on our smartphones, laptops, or televisions. Long-term screen use can cause physical symptoms like eye strain, headaches, and other discomforts. Also, utilizing electronic gadgets right before bed might mess with our sleep cycles and make it more difficult to get to sleep. We can lessen the strain on our eyes and prevent the impacts on our sleep by setting time limits for using these devices.

Getting away from social media and electronic

devices can also boost our creativity and productivity. Notifications and alerts make it simple to become side-tracked, which might stop us from working or being creative. If we reduce our time on these devices, we can concentrate on our work and allow our thoughts to wander, resulting in fresh insights and ideas.

Additionally, setting limits on our use of social media and other digital devices can improve the relationships we have with those around us. While we may be physically present when we're constantly checking our phones or scrolling through social media, our minds are not. The inability to relate to those around us as a result can cause us to feel distant. We can improve the quality of our interactions with others and create deeper, more meaningful connections if we limit the amount of time we spend on these devices.

Journaling

Journaling can help you let go by giving you a place to reflect on your feelings and ideas and identify what you are hanging onto. Journaling enables you to process your emotions without becoming emotionally invested. It can be difficult to look at something objectively when we are deeply involved in it. Our emotions can cloud our judgment and make it hard to make rational decisions.

Journaling can aid by offering a way to recognize patterns and actions that might be keeping you stuck. Without even realizing it, we might be repeating the same patterns and actions. By allowing you to think back on your thoughts and actions over time, journaling can help you become aware of these patterns.

You can break free from these patterns with the aid of this insight and make changes that serve you better. You can openly express your feelings while doing so in a secure environment. You can also acquire perspective and detach yourself from your ideas and feelings by putting them in writing, which may make it simpler for you to separate from circumstances and connections that are no longer beneficial to you.

Furthermore, you can let go of the demand for control through journaling. When we are attached to control, we can become rigid and inflexible in our thinking. We could have difficulty adjusting to change and might be wary of novel concepts or experiences. By enabling you to consider many viewpoints and concepts, journaling can help you break free from this desire. You can improve your ability to think flexibly and with greater openness by taking some time to consider your ideas and beliefs. It can be simpler to embrace change and give up control as a result.

IN THE END, understanding our attachments is basically about understanding who we are and where we fit in the world. By recognizing what we are attached to and why it is important to us, we can build better self-awareness, cultivate stronger relationships, and find greater meaning and purpose in our lives.

However, we must also be aware of the possible drawbacks of attachment and strive to develop a positive relationship with our attachments that enables us to prosper rather than endure suffering. We can create a life that is more satisfying, happier, and more connected to the people and things that matter most if we have a better knowledge of our attachments.

Ultimately, by letting go of our attachment to certain results or expectations, we are able to live more in the present. We can now explore and develop our feminine character by embracing traits like empathy, intuition, and vulnerability. This is the next step in our journey to greater self-awareness and personal growth.

4

Step Three: Grow Into Your Feminine Character

We all possess both masculine and feminine energy as humans. Assertiveness, strength, and independence are traits linked to masculine energy, whereas caring, compassion, and intuition are traits connected to feminine energy. Although these energies are not inherently gender-specific, societal norms often push people to embody one more than the other.

It's imperative to note that a healthy balance of masculine and feminine energy can be beneficial in many different aspects of life. You can develop greater self-assurance, empathy, and success in both personal and professional relationships by striking a balance.

Many girls who are growing up in the 21st century are being raised by mothers in their wounded feminine energy. These women grew up in a time where they had to persevere through extremely limited educational and career opportunities. Because these women pushed themselves so far into their masculine energies to achieve all that they did, they now possess a wounded feminine energy that they unknowingly pass along to their daughters.

These daughters are now taught to fend for themselves and never rely on anyone for anything. Although this idea comes from a valid place and has a reasonable basis around it, many girls end up forgetting to nurture their feminine energy as a result. This trend towards masculine energy is now reinforced by the growing number of educated women who are joining the workforce.

As more women enter traditionally male-dominated occupations, they have to adopt masculine attributes to succeed. They have to be assertive in negotiations, competent in the job market, and intelligent in decision-making. These skills that have helped women break through the glass ceiling and achieve power and influence stand true today.

Nevertheless, as the culture regarding dating and

relationships evolves, women begin to discover that they are constantly struggling to create a balance between their masculine and feminine energy. Women in their masculine energy might find it difficult to lean into their feminine energy when it comes to dating.

This is because while women have acquired more independence and freedom, societal norms and gender roles have not altered as quickly. Women may experience conflicted feelings between their desire for achievement and independence and the traditional standards of femininity. They may feel pressured to be assertive and confident in their careers, while also expected to be loving and accommodating in their relationships.

Therefore, it is challenging for many women to maintain a healthy balance of feminine and masculine energy in their relationships. They may have trouble asserting themselves and communicating their demands, or they might feel guilty about putting their work before their personal lives.

Women aren't the only ones who struggle to strike a balance between masculine and feminine energies. Men are also under societal pressure and find it difficult to express their vulnerabilities and feelings. However, as we women work on balancing our energy, we can help men do the same.

We can start to balance our masculine and feminine energy by recognizing that men and women are both capable of empathy, intuition, and resilience, in addition to being assertive, rational, and ambitious. We must reject the notion that feminine energy is weak and subordinate to masculine energy.

We can start embracing femininity in our daily lives once we have realized its importance. This means creating space to be vulnerable, expressing your emotions, and connecting with your intuition. It also means you are able to establish boundaries and be assertive without sacrificing your femininity.

It is challenging to achieve this balance, but it is necessary for women who wish to lead honest, satisfying lives. It necessitates a readiness to reject conventional gender roles and embrace a different way of being. It also calls for self-acceptance and awareness of oneself, as well as a readiness to be open to risk and vulnerability.

The Downsides of Neglecting Your Femininity

Empathy, nurturing, and sensitivity are all feminine traits. Sadly, modern women have been urged to suppress their such qualities in order to excel in industries where men dominate, or worse, to live up to the current capitalistic standards.

However, there are numerous reasons why women should value their femininity. First of all, femininity is a part of who women are, and ignoring or suppressing this side of themselves can cause feelings of discontent and estrangement. Women can feel more rooted and real in their personal and professional lives by embracing their femininity.

Secondly, in many situations, femininity can be a strength. Leadership roles, interpersonal interactions, and collaborative initiatives can all benefit from traits like empathy, nurturing, and emotional intelligence. Women who embrace their femininity can often be more successful at forming connections and resolving issues at work and can offer a unique viewpoint and skill set to their profession.

Thirdly, embracing femininity does not require women to adhere to conventional gender norms or set limits on their objectives. Instead, it entails embracing and celebrating the full range of their personality and interests, regardless of whether they conform to cultural ideals of femininity or not. Women can be both nurturing and competitive, assertive and empathetic, sensitive and resilient.

Finally, embracing femininity can help challenge and redefine social assumptions related to gender.

When women boldly and truly exhibit their femininity, they can encourage others to do the same and help create a society that is more tolerant and inclusive.

Here are some potential implications of forgetting to nurture your feminine energy.

Burnout

In today's fast-paced society, burnout is a common issue affecting people from all walks of life. But women who prioritize their masculine energy are more likely to experience burnout. Traits that are determined, forceful, and driven by action are examples of masculine energy. While these traits can help people succeed, if they are overused, they can also cause burnout.

Women who prioritize their masculine energy might experience pressure to be "doing" and achieving all the time, which can wear them out emotionally and physically. Society's expectations that women should be able to juggle career, family, and personal life with ease often adds to this pressure. Because of this, many women push themselves to the point of burnout, which can lead to a long period of demotivation and unproductiveness.

Overworking is one of the main factors that can contribute to burnout. When we put our masculine energy first, we often tend to place more emphasis on getting things done than on maintaining our physical and mental well-being. Working long hours, skipping meals, and putting off exercise and self-care can cause persistent stress, exhaustion, and burnout. Furthermore, if we are continually engaged in an activity it can be difficult for us to unwind and disengage from our jobs, resulting in a never-ending cycle of stress and fatigue.

A lack of balance between our masculine and feminine energy is another aspect of burnout. Prioritizing our masculine energy can cause us to disregard our feminine side and feel cut off from our true self. Burnout, worry, and feelings of emptiness can result from this sort of detachment.

In order to avoid burnout, it's crucial to put self-care first; including exercise, a balanced diet, and adequate sleep. Setting boundaries and saying no to tasks that are not necessary or that are beyond our capacity is also crucial. Finding ways to balance masculine energy and foster a sense of wholeness and well-being can also be accomplished by incorporating feminine energy into our lives. This can entail doing something creative, spending time outside, or engaging in mindfulness and meditation.

Difficulty Connecting With Others

Connecting with others is a basic human need that is essential to our general well-being. Establishing emotional relationships with others can be difficult for certain people, especially women who revere their masculine energy. Feminine energy is required to connect emotionally with others. For this reason, women who prioritize their masculine energy find it difficult to develop lasting relationships.

Women in their masculine energy are more likely to embrace traits like assertiveness, competitiveness, and proactive conduct, which may affect their capacity for interpersonal connection. For instance, it could be challenging for others to approach them if they come across as nonchalant and aloof. In addition, women in their masculine energy might find it difficult to understand others' emotions and have trouble empathizing with them. Due to their inability to empathize with others, they may have superficial relationships that lack connection and emotional fulfillment.

Furthermore, women who prioritize their masculine energy may find it challenging to communicate their emotions honestly, which can also lead to difficulty connecting with others. Emotional expression is crucial for establishing meaningful relationships since it promotes mutual trust and intimacy. They also have a hard time expressing vulnerability, which can make it difficult for others to relate to them. Because of this, women in their masculine energy may have a sense of alienation and disconnection from those around them, further exacerbating their difficulty in establishing emotional bonds.

Neglecting Self-Care

Women's physical and emotional well-being can be greatly affected by not taking care of themselves. Many women experience pressure in today's society to put their families, careers, and social life above their own needs. They might therefore neglect to take care of themselves, which could have a variety of unfavorable effects.

Neglecting self-care practices like adequate sleep, a healthy diet, and relaxing activities can result in numerous mental and emotional issues. For instance, sleep deprivation has been linked to impaired cognitive performance, a weakened immune system, and an increased chance of developing chronic illnesses like diabetes and heart disease. Malnutrition, obesity, and cardiovascular disease are among the conditions that can be brought on by poor nutrition. And skipping out on stress-relieving exercises like yoga or meditation might make matters worse, causing stress-related diseases including depression and anxiety disorders.

A woman's relationships with other people may also suffer if she neglects her own needs. Women who don't take care of themselves can get agitated, cranky, and anxious. This can have a detrimental impact on how they interact with friends, family, and coworkers. She might also lose her effectiveness as a caretaker, whether for her young children or elderly parents.

Internalized Misogyny

Internalized misogyny is a phenomenon in which people have unfavorable views toward women and girls as a result of internalizing cultural beliefs about gender roles. Because of pervasive cultural messages that emphasize traditionally masculine traits over traditionally feminine ones, women in particular are susceptible to internalizing misogynism.

In this society that prizes traditionally masculine characteristics, we commonly use the phrase "stop acting like a girl" as an insult. As if being a girl or woman, or having their traits, is supposed to be insulting. This causes girls and women to adhere more to masculine traits and repress their feminine energy. Or worse, they accept the outrageous idea that men are intrinsically better than women.

This can cause them to mistrust their own femininity and lack self-assurance. Women who prioritize their masculine energy could believe that they don't embody the ideal lady society expects or that they aren't "feminine enough." Their self-esteem may suffer as a result, and they may experience feelings of guilt or inadequacy.

Sexist behavior toward other women is another way internalized misogyny can emerge. Women who have internalized misogyny may consider women who value their femininity as weak or inferior and criticize them for not conforming to gender roles, which further perpetuates harmful gender stereotypes.

It is important to recognize and counter internalized misogyny to advance gender equality and empower women. Women should be encouraged to accept all of their positive attributes and reject the idea that some characteristics belong to either men or women.

Furthermore, it is necessary for men to be aware of their own internalized misogyny. Because men have the advantage, it is critical for them to actively speak up and challenge gender stereotypes. By supporting and elevating women, and working to build inclusion, men can play a significant role in advancing gender equality.

Lack of Balance

A healthy and fulfilling existence depends on maintaining balance. When we place one component of ourselves above another, we may lack a sense of harmony and struggle to achieve fulfillment. This is particularly true when it comes to striking a balance between our own masculine and feminine energy. While there is nothing wrong with using your masculine energy, it is crucial to maintain a balance between the two energies to prevent feeling dissatisfied or cut off from your true self.

Both energies are essential for a full and satisfying life. Unfortunately, since societal norms often show a preference for masculine energy (particularly in the workplace), some women prioritize their masculine energy over their feminine energy to succeed in their careers.

It is important to note that when we integrate both energies, we become more adaptive and flexible in how we live, which makes it easier to take advantage of opportunities and handle problems.

However, it is crucial to understand that creating balance does not entail eliminating one energy in favor of another. Instead, it is about incorporating both energies into our lives in a way that feels genuine and fulfilling. This might call for us to change the way we approach particular aspects of our lives, including our careers or relationships. It might also be necessary for us to develop activities like meditation or creative expression that allow us to connect with our feminine energy.

Finally, it's important to remember that there is no one "correct" method to express or balance masculine and feminine energy. Women must recognize the potential consequences of undervaluing their feminine energy and endeavor to find a balance that is comfortable for them.

How to Build a Strong Feminine Character

Women must have a strong feminine character if they are to flourish and succeed in various aspects of their existence. It is a crucial step toward gender equality and the empowerment of women to overcome societal constraints and realize their full potential. A strong feminine character includes not only physical prowess but also mental and emotional fortitude, resiliency, self-assurance, and the capacity to defend oneself and others.

Feminine energy encourages others to follow their intuition, maintains resilience, and knows how to nurture and relate to the people around them. For women to overcome obstacles, lead satisfying lives, and encourage the next generation to do the same, they must develop strong feminine characteristics. Therefore, women who choose to build a strong character can consider the following actions.

Graciousness

Graciousness is often connected with qualities of grace, kindness, and poise. It is the ability to behave towards others in sincere, compassionate, and respectful ways, even in trying circumstances. It requires being willing to extend kindness and charity to those around us as well as demonstrating admiration and respect for others.

Being able to see the good in people is at the core of being gracious. We choose to dwell on their positive traits and strengths rather than their flaws or weaknesses. This has the potential to be an effective tool for developing connections and relationships with others. By valuing and respecting others, we can encourage them to feel the same way about us. This, in turn, can help create an environment favorable to growth and success.

One of the most important aspects of graciousness is being kind and understanding toward others. This means being open to hearing their viewpoints and thoughts and offering support and assistance when they need it. When we act with love and empathy, we create a safe space where people feel at ease about opening up and sharing their thoughts and feelings. This can be especially important in stressful or challenging situations, where people may feel exposed or helpless.

Another key aspect of graciousness is giving freely of our time and resources. When someone is in need or having a hard time, we are willing to lend a hand or offer support and encouragement. Being gracious generates a positive energy that can be particularly valuable in careers or enterprises where networking and developing connections are essential for success.

However, remember that being gracious does not mean being a pushover or enabling others to take advantage of us. Instead, it entails establishing sound limits and standing up for ourselves when necessary. We can clearly and respectfully express our wants and expectations when we behave with grace and poise. This can enable us to forge deep connections with others while also seeing to our own needs.

Generosity

Generosity is a virtue appreciated and promoted in many cultures and faiths around the world. It means offering without expecting a reward. Generosity can take many different forms, like giving money to a charity, giving your time to assist people in need, or just being courteous and kind to others. Generosity, in whatever form, has a tremendous effect on both the giver and the receiver.

Being generous can help you enhance your feminine energy in life. Giving freely to others communicates a sense of compassion and caring for your inner self. This can help you focus on your feminine character and manifest it with confidence and ease. You might start to view your life in a more optimistic light by putting more emphasis on what you have to offer as a caring person.

Also, generosity can promote satisfaction and purpose because giving to others has a positive impact on those who receive it. You are assisting in providing for their needs, easing their suffering, or just bringing joy and happiness into their lives. This sense of purpose and responsibility can be immensely rewarding and make you feel more connected to the world around you.

Furthermore, relationships with others can flourish

through your generosity. Giving volu tarily and freely is an act of kindness, compassion, an empathy. These feminine traits can strengthen your b nds with people and increase your sense of belonging o your community. Furthermore, when you help otl rs, you typically start a cycle of giving that encourage: others to help as well. This might start a chain react n of generosity and goodwill that would make the wo d a better place.

Of course, generosity is not alwa s easy. It can be challenging to give freely when yo are unable to adequately meet your own needs, when you are feeling overburdened or stressed. Ho ever, even small deeds of generosity can have a huge i pact. For example, offering a pleasant word to a str nger, donating a small amount of money to a charity or volunteering for just a few hours can all make a di erence. The key thing is to start where you are and off what you can.

Patience

Patience requires a mental adjustme . It means realizing that diligence and perseverai e are essential components of success, along with itience, because most goals aren't reached overnight. t implies being willing to put in the effort even if the ayoff is delayed, as well as being open to learning f m failures and setbacks encountered along the way.

Those who practice patience are better able to endure challenging circumstances. They understand that success takes time and effort; it is not a race, and the path to prosperity is a process. Even when it seems they are not succeeding, they are prepared to put forth the work. With their perseverance, they are eventually able to get over the obstacles in their way and find the accomplishment they seek.

Also, being patient allows you to keep a long-term perspective instead of getting distracted by short-term ups and downs. This enables you to maintain motivation and keep your sights on the goal, even when progress is slow. Recognizing that setbacks and failures are only temporary obstacles on your path to achievement also helps you avoid being discouraged by them.

Furthermore, being patient requires calling upon your feminine energy and will help you acquire the skills and knowledge required for success. When you have patience, you are willing to put in the time and work necessary to advance your abilities rather than expecting instant results. This gives you the chance to develop a strong foundation of knowledge that will benefit you in the long run. Additionally, because you have the self-assurance that comes from knowing you have worked hard to hone your skills, you can acquire the resilience necessary to recover from setbacks or failures.

Creativity and Innovation

Women have a distinctive perspective that can enhance creativity and innovation. However, they have often been underrepresented in creative industries and leadership roles, which can restrict their impact on the creative process. To increase creativity and innovation, women can accept diversity, build a creative environment, collaborate, and maintain their curiosity.

Expressing oneself creatively can be a powerful way to let emotions out. A safe and productive approach to exploring feelings, thoughts, and experiences is through art, music, writing, and other kinds of creative expression. We can express ourselves in ways that extend beyond words and reach the most intimate parts of ourselves by using our imagination.

It can be cathartic to express oneself through art, whether painting, drawing, or sculpting. It enables us to communicate feelings that we might find difficult to convey verbally and serves as a vehicle for the discharge of repressed emotions like anguish, rage, or frustration. Another potent medium for creative expression is music. Music has the power to arouse powerful emotions and memories, whether we are simply listening to it or performing an instrument. We may not even be aware of our feelings until we release them by playing an instrument.

The key to boosting creativity and innovation is embracing diversity. Women can bring a variety of viewpoints and experiences to the table that might stimulate new mindsets. To actively seek out and value many viewpoints and backgrounds is to embrace diversity. This can involve interacting with people from various cultural, racial, and socioeconomic backgrounds as well as those with various levels of education and work experience. By valuing variety, women can dismantle stereotypes and foster an inclusive environment where everyone feels respected and inspired to share their original ideas.

Therefore, developing a creative environment is crucial for fostering innovation and creativity. Women may nurture creativity by giving room for fresh ideas to flourish, supporting risk-taking, and embracing failure as an essential step in the creative process. Writing is a method of creative expression that can be particularly beneficial in releasing emotions. Writing gives us a secure, private method to process our thoughts and emotions. It can be a method of exploring challenging feelings and experiences as well as a tool for introspection and personal development.

Workshops, training sessions, and mentorship programs are a few examples of learning and development possibilities that can be found in a creative atmosphere. Women may encourage people to think outside the box and take chances by fostering a creative environment, which will result in original solutions and ideas.

Another key element in boosting creativity and innovation is collaboration. Women can work together to share their knowledge, experience, and talents in order to come up with fresh concepts and solutions. Silos may be broken down and a culture of shared learning and creativity can be established through collaboration. Women can develop better networks and relationships that assist them in their creative endeavors by working together.

Finally, fostering creativity and innovation requires maintaining a sense of curiosity. By asking questions, looking into new concepts, and seeking out new experiences, women can develop a mindset of curiosity. Innovative ideas and solutions can result from curiosity, which may not have been conceivable without an open mind and a willingness to explore the unknown. Curiosity is a virtue that can help women evolve as innovative thinkers and leaders.

Empathy and Understanding of Others

Women are often thought to be better at demonstrating greater empathy and understanding than men. This may be due to socialization having a big influence on how gender variations in empathy are shaped. Girls are recognized to have better social skills and a greater capacity to comprehend and relate to others' feelings from a very young age.

In addition to socialization, biological elements may also contribute to gender disparities in empathy. Oxytocin is a hormone linked to social contact and bonding, and studies have shown that women often have higher quantities of it than men do. Women also typically exhibit higher levels of activity in specific brain regions linked to emotional processing and empathy.

Whatever the particular causes of gender disparities in empathy may be, it is undeniable that women are more adept at demonstrating empathy and understanding of others than men. Women are often more perceptive of nonverbal signs and are more adept at reading and understanding body language, tone of voice, and facial expressions. This enables them to behave in a more sympathetic and encouraging manner by picking up on tiny emotional clues that men might overlook.

Women also tend to express themselves more freely and openly, which might make them more personable and approachable to others. In cases where people are coping with harsh emotions or challenging circumstances, this can help to develop tru   and strengthen social ties.

Overall, there are a variety of exp   inations for why women may be more adept than n   n at displaying greater empathy and understanding c   others. Women often have a distinctive set of talents   ind abilities that enable them to connect with people   n a deeper level and to respond to their needs mor   sympathetically and helpfully. These skills and abilitie   may come from socialization, biology, or their appro   ch to problem-solving.

Of course, it is crucial to acknow   dge that not all women are the same and that there   are a variety of personal variations within every gend   group. It's vital to remember that men can exhik   empathy and compassion as well and avoid stereoty   ing or essential-izing gender differences.

However, we can build a more inc   isive society that values empathy, compassion, and und   erstanding if we acknowledge the special skills wom   n bring to the table. We could all benefit from lea   ing to be more sympathetic toward others (in both   ir personal and professional   interactions)   and   a   preciating   the profound influence that women have   n defining what it means to be compassionate people.

Health and Physical Fitness

Women can encounter various problems as they develop their femininity. In an effort to combat this, they can enhance their general well-being and give themselves the confidence to take charge of their lives by prioritizing their health and physical fitness. Regular exercise can be a powerful tool for boosting self-assurance, self-efficacy, and self-acceptance. It can also have considerable positive effects on both physical and mental health. Hence, as women move through different stages of life and work to become their best selves, they should consciously make an effort to prioritize their health and fitness.

Exercise and physical activity are crucial parts of a healthy lifestyle because they have a big impact on overall health and fitness. Regular exercise can lower the chances of developing chronic diseases, including heart disease, stroke, and diabetes. Moreover, it can strengthen bones, increase bone density, and lower the chance of developing certain malignancies. Physical exercise can also assist in strengthening the immune system, reduce inflammation, and enhance mental wellness.

Exercise has also been demonstrated to lessen the signs of depression and anxiety and can assist with mood and general well-being. It can be a potent strategy to enhance mental health or women, who sometimes encounter particular ment l health difficulties such as postpartum depression.

Furthermore, exercise can assist i increasing self-esteem and confidence, which is cruc al for women as they navigate societal expectations a und femininity and appearance. Women who put 10re effort into increasing their physical fitness may el more at ease and secure in their bodies, which ma have a positive impact on other aspects of their lives such as relationships and careers.

Focusing on health and physical tness can be an inspiring experience for women in many ways. It enables them to take charge of thei own health and well-being, which can be a potent too or boosting self-efficacy and self-confidence. Also, it c n promote body positivity and self-acceptance in w nen and make them feel more connected to their boc es.

Women can resist social expectatic is of beauty and femininity by placing a strong empha s on their health and physical fitness. Focusing on heal and fitness can be a way to change the narrative and give women the power to define themselves on their own terms in a society that frequently views wome solely for their outward looks.

Spend Time in Nature

A wonderful approach to disconnect from the worries of daily life is to spend time in nature. We are often overwhelmed with continual stimulation in today's environment, from social media to work emails to the news cycle. Finding tranquil moments in our busy days can be challenging, which can lead to stress and fatigue.

Being in nature allows us to calm down and connect with the natural world, whether strolling through the park or hiking through the mountains. This connection may be immensely calming and grounding, allowing us to disengage from the worries and stressors of our lives.

Nature has a way of putting things in perspective and inspiring mindfulness. Being surrounded by the beauty and size of the natural world might make us more aware of how insignificant our issues and concerns are in the overall scheme of things. This can be immensely humbling and allow us to release our ego-driven worries.

The Power of Sisterhood

This is basically about women helping other women. Society's expectations that women should be rivals rather than allies usually result in women becoming competitively pitted against one another. There are huge advantages when women support each other instead of competing. By helping other women, we build a strong network of allies who can offer one another resources, professional guidance, and emotional support as we work toward our common objectives. By removing obstacles, this network can open doors and present chances that might not have been possible otherwise.

Sisterhoods can offer a secure space for women to support and encourage each other in a world where women are often undervalued and underestimated. Also, it can give women a platform to speak out against injustice and promote change. For instance, the #MeToo movement was sparked by women joining together to share their stories and support one another in the struggle against sexual harassment and abuse.

Sisterhoods can also help women navigate societal expectations and gender norms in addition to building a supportive group. Women often receive advice on how to act, dress, and pursue goals. These demands might be burdensome and restrict a woman's potential. Sisterhood makes it possible to question these expectations and encourages women to challenge gender stereotypes. This can inspire women to follow their goals and objectives regardless of social expectations.

Ultimately, the strength of sisterhood goes beyond just promoting personal growth. Challenging and altering society's assumptions and norms can also bring about systemic change. Women who band together in sisterhood can fight for laws and policies that support gender equality and outlaw unfair behaviors. Also, they can contest cultural narratives that uphold negative stereotypes and gender inequity.

Aim for a Greater Sense of Purpose and Meaning in Life

Much like men, women also search for a sense of direction and significance in their lives. However, women often struggle to achieve their dreams and find their true calling due to societal expectations, cultural norms, and gender biases. Glennon Doyle, a bestselling author, lecturer, and activist, has written extensively about women's need to embrace their authentic selves and pursue their passions. In her book *Untamed*, she exhorts women to let go of society's expectations and reclaim their power by acting on their instincts.

The significance of paying attention to one's inner voice is one of the main points to be taken from *Untamed*. Women are frequently taught to prioritize the wants and needs of others before their own. We are instructed to put our families, partners, and careers first before our own health. However, Doyle contends that women must first learn to pay attention to their intuition and follow their instincts in order to discover their purpose. Deep self-awareness and the guts to disengage from others' expectations is necessary for this.

Women are frequently bashed for showing "too much" emotion, or any signs of weakness for that matter. Doyle maintains, however, that openness is not a sign of weakness but rather of power. Women can develop deeper connections with others and discover significance in their relationships by embracing vulnerability and allowing themselves to be seen. To do this, you must be able to take a chance, put yourself out there, and accept the uncertainty and discomfort that comes with vulnerability.

It is imperative to stress the value of community along with hearing one's inner voice and accepting vulnerability. Women are sociable beings who thrive in interpersonal relationships. Instead of emphasizing competition, we must emphasize collaboration. Doyle contends that women must join a group of supportive, encouraging people who share their values in order to discover their purpose. This community can be found in a variety of settings, including online communities, professional networks, and friendships.

Finding a community, embracing vulnerability, and listening to your inner voice are all important, but they are not sufficient. In addition to all this, women must act and follow their passions. For this, they must be prepared to take chances, fail, and learn from the experience. In order to accomplish their goals, women must be prepared to leave their comfort zones and push past their fears.

By recognizing their desires and acting on them, women who have successfully merged their feminine and masculine energies can develop confidence. They can attract opportunities and experiences that align with their true life path by embracing their distinctive talents and claiming their worth. Practices of self-love and self-care can also strengthen their magnetic energy and, as the next step demonstrates, help them attract abundance in all aspects of their lives.

5

Step Four: Use Your Balanced Energy To Attract Anything

Several elements of our existence, such as our emotions, behaviors, and even our attraction to the things we want, are influenced by energy. Whether we are aware of it or not, the energy we send out into the universe has a big impact on our lives. We can attract everything we want into our lives if we connect our energy with our desires.

Attracting things with energy is a concept upheld by the law of attraction; which implies that we attract the things we focus our energy on, whether positive or negative. Therefore, it's important to have a positive outlook on life and focus on abundance rather than scarcity.

Believing that there is enough of everything to go around is one of the key elements to developing an abundance mindset. This applies to anything we seek, such as money, love, fulfillment, or happiness. We attract more of what we want into our lives when we believe there is an abundance of everything.

Giving ourselves permission to want and receive what we desire is also essential. We often set ourselves up for failure by thinking we don't deserve or can't have something. Yet, if we allow ourselves to want something and feel deserving of it, we may attract it into our lives.

It's also necessary to balance our feminine and masculine energy if we want to attract the things we want. Feminine energy is connected to receptivity, intuition, and creativity, whereas masculine energy is linked to activity, reason, and assertiveness. Combining these energies enables us to reach our full potential and draw more of what we desire into our lives.

Focusing on our thoughts and emotions will help us use our balanced energy to attract anything. We should monitor our thoughts and make sure they align with what we want as this is what creates our reality. If we want to be financially abundant, for example, we should entertain thoughts of abund nce and success rather than scarcity and lack.

Also, our emotions are very influe ial in helping us achieve our goals. Positive emotions l e joy, gratitude, and love help us attract more happy c casions into our lives. Whereas negative feelings, such s anger, distrust, and fear, might drive away what we w nt.

It's important to take inspired a ion toward our aspirations. When we act in a wa that suits our desires, we let the universe know th t we're open to getting what we want. By taking ction, we can strengthen our confidence and create fresh opportunities in our lives.

It's also critical to have faith in the process and trust that our desires will come true. We ca attract more of what we want into our lives by placin our trust in the universe and believing that everythin is happening in our best interests.

Moreover, gaining success in all spheres of life, whether personal or professional, rec ires the conviction that there is enough for eve yone and that, through our ideas and deeds, we can shape the world around us. Developing an abundanc mindset entails putting more emphasis on developme t, opportunities, and possibilities than scarcity, restricti 1, and lack.

In order to change our perspec ve from one of scarcity and fear to one of abundanc and possibilities, we must be more willing to take chances, be kind, and rise to new challenges. Every element of our lives, including our relationships, employment, and finances, is impacted by this optimistic outlook.

Having an abundance attitude can make all the difference in the business world. Entrepreneurs with an abundance attitude are more inclined to take measured risks, perceive possibilities where others see obstacles, and persevere despite losses. They approach these relationships from a perspective of generosity and collaboration, which increases the likelihood that they will forge deep bonds with clients, staff, and partners.

In personal relationships, establishing an abundance mindset can lead to deeper connections and more meaningful interactions. When we believe that there is adequate love, attention, and support for everyone, we are more likely to give freely and receive graciously. In knowing this, we also begin to recognize when a relationship is no longer serving us. Because we believe that there are plenty of connections to be made, releasing a person who is holding us back is made easier than ever. You gain a sense of community, strengthen your valuable relationships, and build a positive cycle of reciprocity by embracing this belief.

Keep in mind that cultivating an abundance mindset requires consistent practice and intentional effort throughout your life. Yet, the advantages of adopting this mindset are monument l and can result in a happier, more satisfying life mark d by success and prosperity in all areas.

Here are some practices to help y 1 succeed in this venture.

Visualization

The process entails using your imagi ation to conjure up vivid mental representations of yo r goals and aspirations, followed by focusing on thos representations to make them a reality. Visualization in be an invaluable tool to help you achieve your g ls, whether you want to be financially successful, lanc your dream job, or strengthen your relationships.

Clearly defining your goals and c eams is the first step in using visualization to attract bundance. This entails being very clear about your g ls and why they are meaningful to you. Spend son : time thinking about your values and priorities, as ell as what you hope to accomplish in the various spl res of your life. You may begin to visualize what it ould be like to attain your goals once you have a clea sense of them.

It's important to have an accura e and complete

mental image when envisioning your goals and desires. This entails imagining how your life would be if you had already accomplished your goal. For instance, if you want to manifest financial prosperity, picture yourself owning a luxurious car, residing in a stunning home, and having the opportunity to travel and follow your dreams.

Using all of your senses will help you visualize your goals more clearly. To do this, you must picture not only what you would see, but also what you would taste, feel, hear, and smell. For example, if you are visualizing yourself on a beach vacation, you might imagine the taste of a cold drink in your hand, the warmth of the sun on your skin, the sound of the waves crashing, the scent of saltwater in the air, and so on.

Visualization is most effective when practiced regularly and consistently. This involves taking time each day to concentrate on your objectives and creating as detailed a mental image of them as you can. To keep your goals at the forefront of your mind all day, you might find it useful to make a vision board or other visual reminder of them.

The ability to change your thoughts and energy to a more positive state is one of visualization's key advantages. Your thoughts and feelings are attracted to chances and resources that can help you achieve your goals when you are emotionally and mentally focused on them.

Developing an attitude of graciousness in your daily life is key if you want to effectively utilize the power of imagination. This means focusing on expressing gratitude and respect for others.

Self-Belief

Believing in yourself is one of the most important traits a person can have. It is the basis for personal growth and success. When a person believes in themselves, they are more likely to take action, be resilient, and succeed in their goals.

Self-belief is the confidence that a person has in their skills, talents, and worth. It is the belief that they can accomplish their goals and overcome any obstacles that stand in their way. When a person believes in themselves they have a sense of self-worth, which is necessary for living a happy and meaningful life.

Language is a powerful tool that can influence our mindset and beliefs. The way we interact with ourselves and others can influence our attitudes and behaviors toward different aspects of life. When it comes to having money, using positive language and affirmations can help support a mindset that attracts wealth and abundance, instead of using negative language that reinforces scarcity and lack.

When it comes to money, one of the most commonly heard negative expressions is "I can't afford that." The idea that money is limited and that one cannot obtain their desires is reinforced by this remark. People may also feel helpless and constrained by their options as a result. But if we alter this language to a positive affirmation, like "I choose not to buy that at this time," we change the emphasis from deficiency to empowerment. This affirmation recognizes that we have power over our financial decisions and a choice in how we spend our money.

Another negative phrase that people often use is "I'll never be able to save enough money." This phrase reinforces a belief that saving money is difficult or unattainable, which can create a sense of hopelessness. Instead, we can rephrase this language into a positive statement, such as "I am capable of saving money, and I am taking steps towards my financial goals." This affirmation reinforces a belief in our own ability to save money and manage our financial future.

Self-belief is not only crucial for personal growth and success, but also improves mental health and well-being. When we believe in ourselves, we are more likely to have a positive attitude toward life and feel more in control of our circumstances. This can result in improved relationships, better physical health, and a greater sense of satisfaction and fulfillment.

On the other hand, a lack of self-belief can be detrimental to our mental health. Anxiety, despair, and substance misuse are all symptoms of low self-esteem and lack of confidence. It can also result in lost opportunities and a sense of regret over not pursuing our aspirations.

Embracing Change

Change is an inevitable part of life, and while it can be frightening and unsettling at times, it also needed for growth and progress. Being open to change is important for developing an abundance mindset, which means being flexible and adaptable in the face of difficulties and opportunities.

By accepting change, we make room in our hearts and minds for fresh insights and experiences. We develop a higher tolerance for failure and a greater willingness to attempt unfamiliar things, both of which can increase our chances of success and fulfillment in our personal and professional lives. Also, resisting change can stifle our potential and keep us back, which stops us from achieving our objectives and fully experiencing life.

One of the secrets to accepting change is to focus

on the opportunities it brings rather than the hardships. The possibility for growth, learning, and self-discovery is present even if change can be challenging and uncomfortable. We may respond to change with a positive outlook and a desire to take on new challenges when we see it as an opportunity to grow and learn.

Moreover, by accepting change, we tend to be receptive to criticism and useful comments. This helps us to obtain important insights and advance ourselves in ways we might not have previously imagined. On the other hand, refusing criticism and holding fast to our own viewpoints can keep us from discovering our blind spots and prevent us from developing as people.

Letting Go of Scarcity

A pervasive mindset of scarcity can prevent people from attaining their objectives and leading satisfying lives. This scarcity mindset is founded on the idea that resources are few and people must compete with one another for them. However, this way of thinking can have a variety of negative effects, such as tension, worry, and even despair. Hence, it is imperative to let go of scarcity and cultivate a mindset of abundance.

The 7 Habits of Highly Successful People by Stephen R. Covey is one book that makes a strong case for the significance of letting go of scarcity. In this book,

Covey makes the case that in order to realize their greatest potential in life, people must change their perspective from one of scarcity to one of abundance. An abundant mindset is built, in Covey's opinion, on the conviction that there is enough for everyone and that one's success does not come at the expense of others.

Covey gives multiple examples of how adopting an abundant attitude can make a person's life better. For example, he talks about the value of an abundance mindset in the workplace. He believes that people who put more emphasis on relationships and collaboration are more likely to succeed than those who adopt a scarcity mindset and see their coworkers as rivals. As people are more likely to share ideas and cooperate to accomplish a common goal, Covey asserts that an abundance mindset can increase productivity, creativity, and innovation.

Additionally, an abundance mindset has positive effects on both one's personal and professional lives. Those who practice abundance are more likely to have satisfying relationships because they are less concerned with attempting to "win" at all costs. Instead, they are able to respect each other's individual abilities and strengths and collaborate to produce results that benefit both parties.

Positive psychology research is increasingly backing

Covey's claim regarding the importance of having an abundance mindset. According to studies, those who enjoy a life of abundance are more likely to feel joyful, grateful, and pleased. They are also able to focus on opportunities rather than obstacles, which makes them more resilient in the face of adversity.

Abundance Mentors

There are plenty of mentors in many aspects of life, including business and entrepreneurship as well as relationships and friendships. One example of an abundance mentor is Oprah Winfrey, who rose from humble origins to become a famous media executive and philanthropist. Oprah has talked about how having an abundance mindset helped her to overcome challenges and accomplish her ambitions. She exhorts others to focus on abundance rather than scarcity and have confidence in their own abilities.

Warren Buffett, a wealthy financier famed for his thrifty way of life and long-term investment methods, is another example of an abundance guru. When it comes to investing, Buffett has stressed the significance of having an abundance mindset and the value of patience, discipline, and a long-term outlook. He also supports charitable giving and has pledged to donate a sizable amount of his money.

Tony Hsieh, the founder of Zappos, is an example of an abundance mentor in the world of entrepreneurship. Hsieh favored developing a workplace culture that respected each person as an individual and placed a high priority on happiness. He believed contented workers would result in contented clients and, ultimately, a prosperous company. Because Hsieh had an abundance attitude, he was able to take calculated risks and think creatively, which helped Zappos succeed and encouraged other entrepreneurs to follow in his footsteps.

Friends and family members that have a positive attitude toward life and support you in your goals might serve as abundance mentors in your personal relationships. A good friend can help you overcome self-doubt and adopt an abundance attitude by encouraging you to take chances and pursue your passions. Similarly, a family member who believes in your goals and provides helpful guidance can be a transformative mentor by giving you the support and tools you need to excel.

Nevertheless, you might find it difficult to seek out abundance mentors, particularly if you are surrounded by people who are negative and unsupportive or who have a scarcity attitude. Yet, there are several ways to locate mentors, including going to networking events, joining professional associations, and looking for mentors via online forums or mentorship programs.

However, it should be kept in mind that when looking for abundance mentors, it's important to look for those who share your beliefs and objectives as well as those who have an optimistic attitude toward life and are ready to help and encourage you. Aside from being open to learning from others, it's also critical for them to be willing to attempt new things, even if it makes them uncomfortable, and to take action.

Embrace Abundance as a Lifestyle

In today's fast-paced society, many of us are consumed by the drive to amass wealth and possessions in pursuit of what we believe is success and pleasure. However, abundance extends beyond material possessions and monetary affluence. Adopting an abundant lifestyle entails viewing the world from a different perspective. One in which we value the abundance that already exists in our lives, and conduct ourselves in a way that draws more of it.

Understanding that there is enough for everyone is a necessary part of living abundantly. There is no need for rivalry or comparison because it is not a zero-sum game. We can admire others' accomplishments without feeling threatened or jealous when we approach life with this mentality. Knowing that their success does not undermine our own allows us to enjoy their accomplishments. Instead of fostering competition and division, this promotes a sense of community.

Ultimately, adopting abundance as a way of life gives up the desire for control. We get a sense of ease and flow when we believe that everything is happening for our greater good, even when we don't know how. When we let go of the need to control every detail of our lives, it fosters our faith that everything will work out the way it is supposed to.

Living abundantly also means concentrating on what we want rather than what we don't want. When we concentrate on scarcity and lack, we attract more of the same since our ideas and beliefs shape our reality. Therefore, when we concentrate on what we desire and see ourselves already having it, we attract wealth into our lives. This is not to mean that we should ignore our problems or difficulties, but rather that we should approach them from a position of abundance and have faith that we will find solutions.

However, it's important to understand that an abundant mindset does not imply that everyone will have access to the same opportunities and resources. People's access to employment, health care, education, and other basic human rights is still hampered by systemic hurdles and inequalities such as institutionalized racism, sexism, ableism, and poverty.

Hence, having an abundance mindset does not mean rejecting or dismissing these barriers and inequalities. Instead, it entails becoming aware of them and taking steps to resolve them. An abundance mindset can empower people and communities to speak out against systems that support injustice and inequality as well as to support laws and procedures that advance equity and inclusion.

This empowerment can be achieved by encouraging people to share their resources, skills, and knowledge with others, especially those who have been historically disadvantaged or excluded. Another strategy is promoting collaboration amongst individuals with various experiences to recognize the value of diversity and inclusion in fostering innovation, growth, and creativity.

Moreover, an abundance mindset can assist people and communities in redefining their understanding of success and achievement. Instead of measuring success solely in terms of money, status, or other material possessions, an abundance mindset promotes personal growth, learning, and contribution to society. This can elicit a more fulfilling and meaningful sense of purpose and can help to lessen the pressure brought on by competitive and individualistic cultures.

Develop Confidence and Improve Decision-Making Skills

Being self-assured and having sound decision-making abilities are more crucial than ever in the fast-paced world of today, as women encounter many obstacles that call for them to act quickly and decisively. Making decisions and having an abundance mindset are crucial talents that can be developed and improved with practice and by studying others' experience.

According to Katty Kay and Claire Shipman's book *The Confidence Code: The Science and Art of Self-Assurance—What Women Should Know*, women frequently lack confidence while making decisions, which can result in a lack of assertiveness and missed chances. Developing self-confidence is one of the first measures women can take to enhance their ability to make decisions.

This entails accepting their flaws as well as their talents, seeing that they are capable of making wise choices, and having confidence in themselves. Women should concentrate on increasing their knowledge and skills, ask for advice and feedback, and take chances even when they are unsure of the results in order to develop confidence.

The habit of overthinking is a serious issue that may impact a woman's ability to make decisions. Women tend to study situations and weigh several possibilities, which can cause them to become indecisive and self-conscious. Women should learn to trust their gut feelings and base their decisions on intuition. This means paying attention to their gut instincts and acting on them without hesitation, even when they lack sufficient evidence to make an informed decision.

Women can further develop their ability to make decisions by learning to prioritize tasks and establish specific objectives in addition to following their intuition. This includes prioritizing their desired objectives and deciding what is most crucial. The authors of *The Confidence Code* advise women to develop delegation skills and learn to let go of things that don't fit with their priorities or skill sets. Women can free up time and energy by delegating work so they can concentrate on the things that matter most.

Finally, women who are able to control their emotions and remain composed under duress can make better decisions. Women usually suffer from higher levels of self-doubt and worry than men, which might impair their capacity for adopting an abundance lifestyle. In order to get past this, women can practice mindfulness, meditation, or other relaxation methods to learn how to control their emotions. In addition, they should learn how to reframe negative ideas and concentrate on the best possible consequences.

Enhance Leadership Abilities

There is still a gender disparity in eadership, even though women have been breaking d wn barriers and reaching greater heights in these pos ions. By honing their talents, gaining confidence, and networking with other women in leadership roles, wo en can improve their leadership capacities. There a e several books available that might assist women in is endeavor, but *Lean In* by Sheryl Sandberg stands out

Lean In explores the difficulties th women experience at work and how they might ove come such difficulties. The book offers helpful sug estions on how women can improve their leadersl p abilities and advance in their careers. The autho is a well-known leader and former COO of Facebook

One of the book's main messages the significance of women taking on leadership ro s and stepping outside of their comfort zones. Accor ng to Sandberg, the expectations society places on wc en, such as the notion that they should be more n turing and less forceful, frequently serve as a bar er to women's advancement. Despite going agai st conventional expectations, Sandberg exhorts wo en to embrace their goals and lean in.

Building a support network is a other significant concept in the book. Together with th value of having a mentor or sponsor, Sandberg emphasizes how crucial it is for women to support one another in their careers. Women should look for mentors and sponsors who can offer advice, encouragement, and chances for progress.

Increase Financial Independence and Career Success

Women who achieve greater financial security and career advancement often go through a character change, becoming more self-assured, assertive, and independent. Financially independent women have more control over their lives and are free to follow their aspirations without being reliant on anybody else. Being financially independent gives them the freedom to follow their passions and principles, whether that be pursuing a job, starting a business, traveling the world, or giving to a cause they care about. Women are also less likely to feel trapped in unsatisfactory relationships or jobs and more likely to make decisions that are in their best interests when they have the financial resources to sustain themselves and their children.

Another way for women to develop an abundance mindset is through professional accomplishments. It can be difficult, but also empowering, for women to overcome gender preconceptions, prejudice, and bias in order to advance in their jobs. When women demonstrate how capable and intelligent they are by overcoming these barriers, they attract the respect and admiration they deserve. Success in the workplace can provide women with identity, purpose, and fulfillment as they use their abilities to progress in their fields.

Women often develop a strong abundance mindset as they achieve financial independence and professional success. This provides women with the ability to handle difficult social and emotional situations effectively. This could include anything from leading a team to settling a wage dispute or simply overcoming personal difficulties. Women who accept and capitalize on abundance are more likely to succeed on their own terms and encourage other women to follow suit.

To be clear, achieving financial security and professional success do not, by themselves, establish a woman's value. Regardless of whether they want to pursue a traditional job or give priority to their families, communities, or creative endeavors, women should be allowed to select their own path and define their own definition of success. Femininity is a multifaceted concept that includes a variety of traits and behaviors, and women should feel empowered to take action and express their femininity in their own special way.

Taking Action

One of the most significant steps to success and abundance in life is taking action toward your goals. It entails overcoming your fear of failing and making the necessary progress toward reaching your objectives. Oftentimes, what makes someone successful or unsuccessful is their capacity for action. There are many examples of women who have taken action to manifest abundance in their lives. Here are just a few examples.

J.K. Rowling

J.K. Rowling, the author of the Harry Potter novels, is an excellent example of someone taking action toward their goals. Rowling was a struggling single mother who had reached her breaking point. She was relying on welfare after losing her job. Despite all this, she vowed not to give up on her goal of becoming a writer.

She devoted all of her spare time to writing the first Harry Potter novel and then sent it to publishers only to receive numerous rejections. But she persisted and was finally accepted by a publisher who was ready to gamble on her. With a net worth of over $1 billion, J.K. Rowling is currently one of the richest novelists in the world.

Sara Blakely

Sara Blakely is the founder of the shapewear brand Spanx, a household name that has transformed the fashion industry. Blakely launched the business with only $5,000 and a desire to offer women ease and confidence in their clothing. Manufacturers repeatedly turned her down, but she persisted. Eventually, she came across a manufacturer ready to take a chance on her and grew Spanx into a well-known brand. As one of the most successful businesswomen in the world, Blakely is now a millionaire.

Melinda Gates

Melinda Gates is an entrepreneur and philanthropist who has devoted her life to serving others. She is a co-founder of the Bill and Melinda Gates Foundation, which has contributed enormous sums of money to programs promoting education and global health. Gates is a fierce supporter of women's rights and has used her influence to bring attention to problems like limited access to healthcare and gender inequality. She has made a big difference in the world by acting on her convictions.

THE ACTIONS of these women are only a few examples of how doing something can lead to outstanding success and positive change. It's essential to continue moving forward, make progress toward your goals, and let go of scarcity despite any difficulties or roadblocks you may encounter.

Finally, even though an abundance mindset is a powerful tool for personal and societal change, it should not be viewed as a panacea for the structural injustices that exist in our society. Rather, it is a complement to social justice and equality and can encourage greater collaboration, generosity, and innovation in our common quest for a more just and equitable world.

Life is a journey of continual growth and evolution, and it's up to us to choose whether we want to keep moving forward or remain static. With the power of choice, we can decide to embrace change and continue evolving until we reach our optimum potential. The final step on this journey of transformation is to stick to this path and always strive for progress.

6

Step Five: Don't Ever Stop Evolving

Humans are made for growth and evolution. We all possess a strong drive to constantly develop into better versions of ourselves with each passing day. But many things, including fear, complacency, and even laziness can sometimes stifle this desire. We must endeavor to continuously grow and seek improvement in all facets of our lives if we want to attain our full potential.

The power of choice is one of our most effective tools as we move toward evolution. We have a plethora of choices every day, including what to eat, how to dress, how to spend our time, who to spend it with, and many others. Even if some of these decisions appear trivial, they all have the power to profoundly influence our lives. We prepare ourselves for a life of continuous evolution and self-improvement by deliberately choosing to make positive, growth-oriented decisions every day.

The necessity of engaging in mental, physical, and spiritual activity is an integral part of evolution. Our minds require mental exercise to sustain focus and clarity, just as our bodies require physical activity to keep healthy and strong. Mental exercise can take the form of reading, picking up new skills, engaging in creative activities, or simply pushing ourselves to think beyond our comfort zones. Likewise, our souls require spiritual activity to remain nourished and content as well. This can take the form of relaxation techniques like meditation, prayer, volunteer work, or just being in tune with the natural environment.

Putting our health and well-being first is a critical element of the evolutionary process. The proverb "you are what you eat" is accurate since what we consume directly affects both our physical and emotional well-being. We can energize our bodies and minds more effectively by making deliberate decisions to eat wholesome, nourishing foods. This can also apply to other areas of our lives, including gettir enough sleep, taking care of ourselves, and priorit ing our mental health.

Living a more contented, meanin, ul life ultimately comes down to the decision to never op evolving. We give ourselves access to a world of nitless potential and possibilities when we conscioush choose to grow and improve. We improve our capacit for coping with obstacles and opportunities by beco ing more tenacious, flexible, and well prepared. A ;o, we motivate people close to us to follow our exan le, leading to a positive change that spreads throughc t our communities and beyond.

Naturally, evolution does not alwa ; follow a simple or direct path. There will be difficulti and failures, as well as times of uncertainty and dou t. We can overcome these obstacles and become stronger if we embrace the power of choice and dec ate ourselves to growth. It is a trip that calls for en rance, tenacity, and a strong sense of purpose—but one that is well worth the effort.

Here are some strategies for gettin started.

Read Books and Educate Yourself

One of the most significant aspects of developing oneself is reading and learning new things. Your perspective can be broadened and new opportunities opened by participating in mental challenges that teach you valuable information and skills. There are a variety of ways to increase your knowledge and sharpen your cognitive talents, including reading books, attending seminars, and engaging in other learning activities.

Reading provides an abundance of knowledge and insights on a variety of subjects, including (but not limited to) business, history, science, and personal growth. Reading may boost your vocabulary, develop your critical thinking abilities, and spark your imagination. It's a terrific way to relax and unwind while learning new things.

Another way to learn new information is by attending seminars. Seminars give attendees the chance to hear from experts in a given industry and discover new perspectives and trends. They give you the ability to network with other professionals and learn fresh viewpoints on various problems. There are seminars available on a variety of subjects, such as business, personal growth, health, and wellness.

Fresh knowledge can also be acquired by participating in mental challenges. For example, exercises like taking up a new hobby, learning another language, or actively participating in a community education program can improve your cognitive talents, inventiveness, and self-assurance. They also offer a chance to socialize and make new acquaintances

Learning new activities can also keep your mind active as you age. According to studies, taking part in mentally challenging activities can help delay cognitive aging and lower the risk of dementia. You may remember things better and process information faster.

Explore New Hobbies and Activities

Starting a new hobby or pastime can be an excellent way to push yourself and encourage personal development. There are various activities you can choose from that can help you achieve your goals, whether you're trying to learn a new skill, discover a new passion, or simply find something enjoyable to do with your time.

One of the main advantages of taking up a new hobby or activity is that it offers a healthy way to step outside your comfort zone. It can be disturbing to push yourself to learn something new, but it can also be very rewarding. You might find skills and abilities you didn't know you had by overcoming your anxieties and trying something new, which can be a very powerful confidence booster.

Taking up a new hobby can also be a great opportunity to broaden your social network and meet new people. You're likely to meet people who share your interests if you join a club, take a class, or go to events focused on your hobby. These new relationships can serve as an invaluable support system while you discover your new interest and can keep you motivated when things get tough.

Besides the benefits for personal development, finding a new hobby can be a refreshing diversion from the stresses of daily life. Taking part in an enjoyable activity can be a terrific way to lower stress, improve your mood, and enhance your general sense of well-being. There is a pastime out there for everyone, whether you favor more active pursuits like hiking or yoga, or more artistic ones like writing or painting.

Stay Physically Active

For the sake of your overall well-being and health, it's imperative to stay physically active. The numerous physical and mental benefits of regular exercise include enhanced mood and cognitive function, reduced risk of chronic diseases, increased muscular strength and flexibility, and better cardiovascular health.

There are many different types of exercise to select from, so it's important to find one yo like and can fit into your daily routine. Running, alking, cycling, swimming, and yoga are all fantastic options that can be adapted to suit your preferences an fitness level.

Running is a high-impact exer se that can be performed almost anywhere. It h ps to increase stamina, burn calories, and enhan cardiovascular health. To add running to your dai schedule, start with short distances and gradually i rease the duration and intensity.

Walking is easy on the joints, aking it a low-impact activity that people of all ness levels can benefit from. It's an effective method enhance mood, lower stress, and improve blood circu tion. Try going for a quick walk after supper or d ing your lunch break.

Cycling is another low-impact exe cise that's excellent for improving overall health. It i a versatile exercise choice as it can be done outdoor or indoors on a stationary bike. Try cycling to work o running errands on your bike.

Low-impact exercises like swimm ng are excellent for those with joint problems or inj ies. It's a great way to increase flexibility, muscle stre gth, and cardiovascular health. Try swimming laps your neighborhood pool or incorporating water aerobics into your exercise program.

Yoga is wonderful for enhancing balance, strength, and flexibility. It's a very relaxing, low-impact activity that can ease tension and encourage rest. Try taking a yoga class at your neighborhood gym or studio or watching a yoga video online.

Regular exercise doesn't have to take a lot of time or be difficult to fit into your daily schedule. Set small starting goals before slowly increasing the duration and intensity of your workouts. Always check with a health-care professional before beginning a new workout plan, especially if you have any underlying medical concerns, and be sure to listen to your body and take breaks when needed.

Create a Consistent Schedule

A daily plan can be a fantastic tool for increasing productivity and achieving your objectives. Your physical and mental health can be enhanced by scheduling time each day for exercise, meditation, and a nutritious diet. Here's how to create a daily plan with these important activities on it.

First, decide what time you want to wake up every day. Your schedule will be built around this. To create a regular sleeping pattern, try to wake up at the same time every day, including weekends.

Next, schedule a workout period. According to the Centers for Disease Control and Prevention, adults should engage in at least 150 minutes of moderate-intensity exercise or 75 minutes of vigorous-intensity activity each week. Put this on your schedule after dividing it into daily increments. This could be going for a morning run or walk, attending a fitness class in the evening, or visiting the gym during your lunch break.

After working out, make time for meditation or mindfulness exercises. Studies have shown that meditation can lessen stress and anxiety, improve focus, and boost emotions of well-being. Daily meditation for just a few minutes can have a significant impact. You can use this time to sit quietly and concentrate on your breathing, or you can use a guided meditation app to get started.

Last but not least, schedule time for a healthy meal. To ensure that you have healthy options available all day, plan your meals and snacks in advance. Make sure to consume an abundance of fruits, veggies, lean protein, and nutritious grains. You could also consider setting a fixed time for meals and snacks to control your appetite and avoid overeating.

Make sure to give yourself time to rest and

recharge during the day by taking breaks. This could include going for a brief stroll outdoors, reading a book, or doing something else you want to do. You should also be flexible when planning your day. If you occasionally need to modify your routine, don't be too hard on yourself. Making time for the things that support your health and well-being is crucial.

Try New Foods and Experiences

As people, we all have different tastes and preferences when it comes to food and experiences. However, sticking to familiarity and what we're comfortable with can limit our growth and hinder our ability to widen our perspectives. Trying new foods and experiences can be an incredibly effective way to evolve as a person and gain fresh insights about the world around us.

One of the most logical reasons to try new foods and experiences is the opportunity to broaden our palates and cultural awareness. Food is an inherent part of culture, and exploring the cuisines of different cultures can help us gain a deeper understanding and respect for their traditions and way of life. Whether it's trying sushi for the first time, savoring traditional Indian curries, or experimenting with exotic fruits and vegetables, stepping outside of our culinary comfort zones can be a revitalizing experience.

Trying new meals can be a great approach to challenging our preconceptions and expanding our cultural horizons. Whether we are aware of them or not, we all have implicit biases, and sampling different meals can aid in identifying and overcoming them. For instance, a person who has never loved spicy cuisine may discover that they like the rich flavors of a dish that contains spicy curries or chili peppers. We can enhance our perspectives on new opportunities and experiences by testing our presumptions about what we enjoy and dislike.

Traveling to new places, in particular, can be an incredibly enlightening experience. By immersing ourselves in unfamiliar cultures and environments, we can gain a fresh perspective on our own lives and interests. Whether it's climbing the mountains of Nepal, exploring the streets of Tokyo, or just visiting a new city or town, travel can help us break out of our routines and view the world with refreshed eyes.

Of course, attempting unfamiliar meals and activities might be intimidating, particularly if we're used to sticking to what we know. But moving outside of our comfort zones is a crucial part of evolving personally. It's normal to feel uneasy or unsure while trying something new, but by getting through these emotions, we can expose ourselves to fresh opportunities and experiences.

Starting small can help make trying new foods and activities less scary. For instance, if you've never tasted Thai food before, start with a simple dish like Pad Thai and work your way up to more complex flavors and dishes. Likewise, if you're hesitant to visit a foreign country, start with a nearby location or plan a guided trip to help you get used to the experience.

Seek Feedback

Asking for feedback from trusted friends or mentors is one of the most effective methods of personal development. Feedback can give us valuable insights into areas for growth that we may not have been aware of and helps us understand how others perceive us. Friends or trusted mentors can offer a fresh viewpoint on our talents and flaws. They may provide us with helpful criticism that will allow us to improve. These people are often able to offer frank criticism that might be unsettling to hear but is ultimately rewarding.

It's crucial to choose people who will give us honest, constructive criticism and have our best interests at heart when asking for feedback. This can include intimate friends, coworkers, family members, and even mentors in the workplace. These people should understand our goals and be reliable and deserving.

When seeking feedback, it's crucial to enter the conversation with an open mind and the readiness to accept any kind of feedback, even if it's negative. To ensure we fully understand the feedback being delivered, we should pay close attention and take notes. It's also necessary to clarify any issues that might be unclear or confusing by asking questions.

After receiving feedback, we should pause to think about what was said and how we can use the advice to improve ourselves. We should decide which areas require improvement and develop a strategy for doing so. It's crucial to follow up with our mentors or friends to let them know how we've used their advice and to request more help or direction if necessary.

In addition to seeking feedback from trusted mentors and friends, it's crucial to give back to the people who come to you for feedback in order to maintain a positive, empowering cycle. This should always be done in a respectful and constructive way by being explicit, emphasizing actions over personal traits, and making suggestions for improvement. We can help others progress and better themselves by providing useful and encouraging feedback, just as our mentors and friends have given us.

Maintain a Sense of Humor

Maintaining a sense of humor and enjoying yourself along the way can be an effective strategy to succeed in life. While many people believe that personal growth needs a tight focus on goals and objectives, it's important to remember that laughter and play can be just as crucial.

Humor and fun lower stress and enhance mental health, which is one of the reasons they are so important. People who are overly focused may experience anxiety or become overwhelmed, which could inhibit their progress. But people can lower their stress levels and enhance their general well-being by finding methods to add humor and playfulness to their lives. This can encourage people to approach their objectives in a more optimistic and successful manner.

Moreover, the ability to laugh at oneself and have a sense of humor could be signs of emotional intelligence. Those who are able to find humor in events and take themselves less seriously are frequently better able to handle setbacks and failures. They are able to move on more swiftly after setbacks, which is a crucial skill for success in any field.

Also, having fun and maintaining a positive outlook can make work more enjoyable, which can result in higher productivity and success. When people are engaged in work they enjoy, they are more likely to put in the time and effort necessary to succeed. A better sense of happiness and contentment can result from this, as well as increased creativity and invention.

Of course, finding the right balance between having fun and achieving one's objectives is important. While it's necessary to unwind and enjoy life, it's equally crucial to maintain commitment and concentration on your goals. Nevertheless, people can maintain an acceptable balance between work and play by finding methods to include humor and play in their daily routines.

One way to maintain a sense of humor and have fun is to surround yourself with positive people who share your sense of humor and interests. Spending time with friends and colleagues who can make you laugh and appreciate the lighter side of life can be an excellent way to reduce stress and stay motivated.

To add humor to your life, you should learn to laugh at yourself. Making light of your own errors and failings can be a terrific approach to reduce tension and stay grounded. Individuals can avoid becoming overly defensive or self-critical, which can impede progress, by being overly concerned about their own flaws.

Discover Success

You can reach your entire potential and attain your desired level of success by embracing the concept of evolution. Success is a journey, not a destination, and that must always be kept in mind. It calls for tenacity, commitment, and the readiness to grow from mistakes. You can achieve remarkable things and realize your potential if you have the correct perspective, attitude, and work ethic.

Moreover, when considering the subject of self-evolving, it's important to understand the meaning of success. Success is the execution of a desired outcome or purpose, and it is strongly tied to self-evolving because it includes continuous growth and improvement.

Stephen Covey's book, *The 7 Habits of Highly Successful People*, addresses how self-evolving and success work hand in hand. Covey places a strong emphasis on self-improvement and the connection between values and objectives to succeed. He argues that self-evolving is essential for both personal and professional success.

However, success is a very personalized and challenging concept, and it's commonly misunderstood to be a final destination rather than a never-ending journey. It is not a permanent place that one can arrive at and then just remain in forever. Success is a continuous process that calls for effort, perseverance, and a readiness to adapt to changing circumstances.

Many people think of success as materialistic or financial accomplishment, but in truth, success can include personal development, self-actualization, and having a positive impact on the world. Success is assessed by internal factors like satisfaction, fulfillment, and happiness, in addition to external factors like wealth or recognition.

Self-discovery is the first step on the road to success. Understanding one's skills, assets, liabilities, and interests is important. Those who are aware of themselves are better able to develop objectives that are in line with their values and strengths. Self-discovery provides people with clarity and direction as they establish their mission in life. It is a journey of introspection that allows individuals to analyze their attitudes, habits, and beliefs.

Here are some strategies to aid you on your journey to self-discovery and success. Whether you're just starting out or looking to make a change, these strategies will empower you to take charge of your life and achieve the success you deserve.

Remind Yourself of Your Strengths

Focusing on your strengths is an important aspect of personal and professional growth. This strategy emphasizes recognizing, honing, and utilizing your innate talents, abilities, and skills, rather than obsessing over your weaknesses. By honing your strengths, you can improve your performance, output, and satisfaction in all aspects of your life.

The ability to succeed in areas where you have a natural aptitude or talent is one of the main reasons for concentrating on your strengths. Focusing on your strengths increases your chances of success and enjoyment, which motivates you and piques your interest in what you do. On the other hand, if you concentrate on your shortcomings, you could find it difficult to advance, feel overburdened, and go through frustration and burnout.

You can boost your confidence and self-esteem by concentrating on your strengths. You will feel more secure in your skills and more self-assured in your decisions when you succeed in areas where you are naturally gifted or talented. You can conquer hurdles, take calculated risks, and welcome new challenges if you have confidence, which translates into a positive attitude.

Concentrating on your strengths also makes it

possible for you to make significant contributions to society. You can have a positive impact on people and the world around you by utilizing your abilities. For instance, if you have a talent for communication, you might be an expert at writing or public speaking, which can motivate and instruct others. Strong analytical abilities can help you succeed in research or data analysis, which informs and guides decision-making. Whatever your strengths are, there is always a useful and effective method to put them to use.

However, it's crucial to remember that focusing on your strengths does not mean ignoring your weaknesses. For personal and professional success, acknowledging and addressing your weaknesses is also important. By identifying areas where you need improvement, you can develop plans to overcome them or enlist support from others who are experts in those areas. However, the key is to view your shortcomings as opportunities for growth, rather than limitations on your potential.

Looking back on your previous experiences and achievements is one way of identifying your strengths. Try to pinpoint the underlying qualities and abilities that helped you succeed as you reflect on the pursuits, assignments, or tasks that you found enjoyable and succeeded at. You can also elicit opinions about your abilities from others, including coworkers, friends, and family. Take a strengths assessment, such as the CliftonStrengths assessment, as an alternative strategy. This tool identifies your top five strengths and offers advice on how to make the most of them.

Once you have discovered your strengths, it's important to develop them further. This can include looking for chances to put your skills to use in different situations, like taking on new challenges or offering to fill leadership roles. It could also entail looking for mentors or coaches who can help you develop your strengths and offer advice and assistance.

Accept Challenges

Life is a series of challenges that must be faced and overcome in order to grow and become successful. Personal hardships and professional obstacles are only two examples of the many different types of challenges that might arise. Nevertheless, we often attain our greatest successes as a result of struggling through the most difficult situations.

Viewing problems as opportunities for development and learning is one of the secrets to success. Successful people aren't afraid to take risks or deal with uncomfortable situations. Instead, they're eager to leave their comfort zones and take on tasks that others would find intimidating.

By taking on problems, we give ourselves the chance to encounter new opportunities. We enhance confidence in our skills and acquire important knowledge that can help us excel in every aspect of our lives. Whether we succeed or fail, every challenge we face offers us insightful feedback that we can use to develop as people and become better suited to handle challenges in the future.

Taking on challenges has advantages in your personal life as well as your career. Those who are prepared to take on difficult initiatives and activities are increasingly sought after by employers. People that fit this description are seen as self-starters who approach their jobs with initiative and don't mind taking chances. As a result, they frequently receive rewards like promotions, pay increases, and other opportunities for career progression.

Here are examples of a few of the many women who have achieved success in life by accepting challenges. Their success stories show that achievement requires more than simply talent or knowledge; it also requires the ability to face challenges head-on and persevere through hardship. These women prove that success is achievable if you're prepared to work hard and never give up, even if you face challenges such as discrimination, physical constraints, or setbacks.

Ada Lovelace

English mathematician and author Ada Lovelace is renowned for her innovative contributions to the field of computer science. Lovelace, who was born in 1815, was raised by intellectuals in a mathematical and scientific household. When she first met Charles Babbage, the creator of the Analytical Engine, in 1833, she was enthralled by the machine's potential.

Lovelace persisted and became the first computer programmer in history despite having to live in a culture where men predominated and women were discouraged from pursuing scientific jobs. She created the original algorithm for Babbage's Analytical Engine, widely regarded as the first computer program ever created. She continues to serve as a role model for women in science and technology.

Michelle Obama

During her time as the first lady of the United States, Michelle Obama, the wife of former US President Barack Obama, broke down barriers and confronted prejudice. Michelle, who was the first African-American woman to hold the position, was subject to a great deal of scrutiny and criticism, but she never faltered in her dedication to fighting for issues lik women's rights, health, and education.

Michelle gained international rec gnition as a role model for women and girls. She enc uraged them to achieve their aspirations and never gi e up in the face of difficulty through her work as an dvocate and her compelling public speaking. Mill ns of people continue to be inspired by her grace, it, and fortitude, making her a genuine icon of our day

Angela Merkel

A notable politician, Angela Merk once held the office of Chancellor of Germany. Sh was Germany's first woman head of state and on of the longest-serving heads of government in the w ld.

Merkel is well-known for her lead rship during the Eurozone crisis and her part in han ling the refugee problem. She persevered and rose t the top of her field despite encountering political nd gender bias throughout her career. Merkel is r owned for her cautious, pragmatic approach to poli cs and ability to bring disparate groups together. Both n Germany and internationally, her legacy will be felt r years to come.

Greta Thunberg

Greta Thunberg is a Swedish environmental activist who has attracted attention from all over the world for her work addressing climate change. Thunberg has sparked a worldwide movement of young activists and brought attention to the critical need for immediate climate action while receiving criticism and abuse from politicians and skeptics of climate change.

Greta Thunberg launched the Fridays for Future Movement, organized worldwide climate strikes, and spoke to world leaders at the UN Climate Action Summit. Inspiring millions of people to take action and demand significant change from governments and companies, Thunberg has become a symbol of youth activism and ecology. Her passionate advocacy has inspired a new generation of climate activists to speak openly about the climate crisis.

Indra Nooyi

Indra Nooyi is a trailblazing corporate CEO who has broken down barriers related to gender and culture in the workplace. As a woman of color, she worked her way up to become CEO of PepsiCo, one of the biggest food and beverage corporations in the world, where she revolutionized the business and oversaw creative tactics.

The emphasis on sustainability, healthy products, diversity, and inclusion that Nooyi brought to her leadership was remarkable. She gained widespread acclaim for her dedication to social responsibility, and under her direction, PepsiCo developed into one of the most ecologically responsible businesses in the entire world. Nooyi's legacy serves as proof of the ability to overcome challenges and effect positive change through perseverance, leadership, and persistence.

Jane Goodall

Well-known primatologist and conservationist Jane Goodall devoted her life to learning about chimpanzees and fighting for their preservation. Her groundbreaking 1960s research in Tanzania, where she observed and recorded the intricate social behavior of wild chimpanzees, challenged the dominant scientific theory that only humans are capable of utilizing tools and displaying emotions.

We now have a much better grasp of animal behavior and conservation thanks to Goodall's painstaking research and unconventional method of studying animals in their natural habitat, despite resistance from the scientific community. Generations of scientists and activists have been motivated by her work to take action to save endangered species and their habitats.

———————

WOMEN like these are an inspiration to the world because they have shown that anything is possible with determination and hard work. They have succeeded in breaking through barriers and shattering stereotypes, paving the way for future generations. Their courage and resilience inspire others to pursue their dreams and make a positive impact on the world.

Conclusion

For women who want to empower themselves by embracing their real feminine nature, *The Feminine Empowerment Plan* is an instructive guide. I've clearly stressed throughout the book how crucial it is to let go of the cultural ideals of the perfect woman and unlearn perfectionism in order to live a more balanced and satisfying life. Throughout the book, you have been presented with useful skills for cultivating detachment, developing your feminine energy, using the law of attraction to your advantage, and embracing the never-ending journey of personal evolution.

The idea of a perfect woman is a culturally formed ideal that is often promoted by the media and societal standards. It's critical to understand that such an ideal is unattainable and may even be harmful to women's mental and emotional well-being.

We need to recognize and value the diversity and special qualities of every single woman rather than aiming for an unattainable ideal. There is no such thing as a flawless woman; instead, the world is filled with many amazing and accomplished women who provide different perspectives and strengths.

It's important to realize that perfectionism can be a double-edged sword that both motivates us to do great things and also leads to a great deal of worry and anguish. Realistic goals must be set, failures must be accepted as opportunities for growth, and perfectionism must be unlearned.

Even though it may not be easy to do, letting go of perfectionism can be freeing and result in a life that is more satisfying. We can escape the grip of perfectionism and appreciate the beauty of our flaws if we have patience, perseverance, and the courage to learn from our mistakes.

Another topic I've brought up in the book is practicing detachment. To do this, we must disengage from our attachments and let go of our urge to be in control. By doing this, we can achieve greater inner freedom and peace and improve our ability to make thoughtful, unbiased decisions.

Nevertheless, keep in mind that detachment is

not about being aloof or uncaring; rather, it is about striking a balance between having strong emotions and not letting them control us. Letting go of our expectations and judgments can enable us to establish stronger connections with people and assist us in overcoming anxieties and limiting beliefs.

The concept that you can develop your feminine character by balancing both energies offers important insights into personal growth. Although the idea of balancing masculine and feminine energies is not new, the emphasis on accepting both elements of who we are is crucial.

We can access our creativity, intuition, and empathy by accepting and valuing our feminine attributes. At the same time, we can develop our masculine side, which can make us more focused, determined, and assertive.

Also, developing an abundance mindset is a powerful tool for succeeding in life and finding happiness. We can cultivate a positive attitude that attracts abundance into our lives by switching our focus from scarcity to abundance.

My strategies place a strong emphasis on the value of being grateful, visualizing the life we want, and taking inspired action. We may cultivate an abundance mindset that attracts more of what we already have by acknowledging and appreciating the abundance that already exists in our lives.

Gaining control of an abundance mindset teaches us to let go of limiting thoughts and self-talk that prevent us from realizing our full potential. We can live a life of abundance in all aspects including love, wealth, and happiness, by accepting abundance as a natural state of being.

I have stressed the importance of continuous evolution and the fact that people should never stop changing. I firmly believe that people have the power of choice, which gives them the ability to decide what to do and how to do it in order to influence their destiny. People can change and develop to their full potential by deciding to learn, grow, and develop.

Moreover, be aware that evolution involves more than simply personal development it also entails adjusting to change and remaining relevant in a rapidly changing world. Those who refuse to evolve risk falling behind and missing out on opportunities.

As a result, it's crucial to welcome change, seek out novel experiences, and push oneself to evolve and grow continually. People can achieve new levels of success and fulfillment in both their personal and professional lives by exercising their power of choice and willingness to learn.

Now that you have finished reading *The Feminine*

Empowerment Plan, you've taken a significant step towards creating a more empowered and fulfilling life. But don't let your journey end here. You're still capable of accomplishing so much more!

Now that you have all the tools, go out into the world and use them. Don't let fear or uncertainty stop you from moving forward. It's time to recognize your true potential and build the life you desire. Whether you want to start your own business, strengthen your relationships, or simply discover true happiness and purpose, the power is in your hands.

But keep in mind that you don't have to journey alone. Tell others about your newfound wisdom and motivation. Spread the word about women's empowerment and inspire those around you. We can all benefit from a better, more equitable future if we work together.

And if you enjoyed the book, do leave a review on Amazon. Your feedback is very valuable in letting other readers know about the book. It will also give me the motivation to write more books about the empowerment of women. So let's empower and encourage as many people as we can!

Now go forth, own your power, and build the life you've always wanted. *The Feminine Empowerment Plan* is only the start of the process.

References

Brown, B. (2012). *Daring greatly: How the courage to be vulnerable transforms the way we live, love, parent, and lead.* Penguin Random House.

Brown, B. (2010). *The gifts of imperfection: Let go of who you think you're supposed to be and love who you are.* Hazelden Publishing.

Covey, S. R. (2004). *The 7 habits of highly effective people: Powerful lessons in personal change.* Free Press.

Doyle, G. (2020). *Untamed.* The Dial Press.

Dweck, C. S. (2006). *Mindset: The new psychology of success.* Random House.

Goddard, N. (1952). *The power of awareness.* The Crown Publishing Group

Hollis, R. (2018). *Girl, wash your face: Stop believing the lies about who you are so you can become wi you were meant to be*. Thomas Nelson.

Kay, K., & Shipman, C. (2014). *he confidence code: The science and art of self-assurance—V hat women should know*. HarperBusiness.

Lao Tzu. (n.d.). *Tao te ching* (Tra islated by J. H. McDonald). Shambhala.

Lyubomirsky, S. (2008). *The how oj happiness: A scientific approach to getting the life you want.* N v York: Penguin Press.

Mayo Clinic. (n.d.). *Mindfulness ercises: 10-minute guided meditation.* Retrieved fron https://www. mayoclinic.org/healthy-lifestyle/cons\ ner-health/in-depth/mindfulness-exercises/art-200⁴ :356

Neff, K. D., & Germer, C. K. (⁢)19). *The mindful self-compassion workbook: A proven way to :cept yourself, build inner strength, and thrive*. The Guilford P ss.

Palmer, A. (2019). *The art of askin, How I learned to stop worrying and let people help*. Hachette JK.

Ruiz, D. M. (1997). *The four agr ments: A practical guide to personal freedom*. Amber-Allen Pi)lishing.

Saujani, R. (2019). *Brave, not perfect Fear less, fail more, and live bolder*. Currency.

Schopenhauer, A. (2004). *On wom (Über die Weiber)* (R. J. Hollingdale, Trans.). Penguin Cl ssics.

Wolf, N. (1991). *The beauty myth*. C itto & Windus.

Zander, R. S., & Zander, B. (2000). *The art of possibility: Transforming professional and personal lif*e. Penguin Books.